the Catholic Classics II

Dinesh D'Souza

Preface by Cardinal Bernard F. Law

Our Sunday Visitor Publishing Division
Our Sunday Visitor, Inc.
Huntington, Indiana 46750

Acknowledgments

I wish to thank Susannah McClellan for typing the manuscript and offering helpful suggestions; Mary Murphy for research and editorial help; Michael Novak and Tanya Novak for thoughtful criticism; and Bob Lockwood, publisher and editor in chief at Our Sunday Visitor, for encouraging me to write this book.

Scripture texts contained in this work are taken from the *Revised Standard Version Bible, Catholic Edition*, © 1965 and 1966 by the Division of Christian Education of the National Council of the Churches of Christ in the U.S.A., and used by permission of the copyright owner. Other sources from which material has been excerpted or has served (either quoted verbatim or paraphrased) as the basis for portions of this work include standard versions of the various Catholic classics, among them *History of the Church*, © 1965 by Penguin Books, Middlesex, England; *Proslogion*, © 1965 by Oxford University Press, Oxford, England; *Dark Night of the Soul*, © 1959 by Image Books, Doubleday & Co., Inc., Garden City, N.Y.; and *Mere Christianity*, © 1943 by Macmillan Publishing Co., Inc., New York, N.Y. If any copyrighted materials have been inadvertently used in this book without proper credit being given, please notify Our Sunday Visitor in writing so that future printings of this work may be corrected accordingly.

International Standard Book Number: 0-87973-423-X
Library of Congress Catalog Card Number: 86-61500

Cover design by Rebecca J. O'Brien

PRINTED IN THE UNITED STATES OF AMERICA

For my brother, Shashi,
and my sister, Nandini

CONTENTS

Preface by Bernard Cardinal Law   **5**

1   **Eusebius's Ecclesiastical History**   **7**

2   **Benedict's Monastic Rule**   **25**

3   **Anselm's Proslogion**   **45**

4   **John of the Cross's Dark Night of the Soul**   **62**

5   **Teresa of Ávila's Autobiography**   **77**

6   **Ignatius of Loyola's Spiritual Exercises**   **93**

7   **Robert Bellarmine's Controversies**   **112**

8   **Thérèse of Lisieux's Story of a Soul**   **133**

9   **Jacques Maritain's Integral Humanism**   **151**

10   **C.S. Lewis's Mere Christianity**   **166**

preface

IN this much-awaited sequel, Dinesh O'Souza returns to that format which he uses so well in the first part of *The Catholic Classics*. The approach of Mr. D'Souza is straightforward and as a result very useful for the reader who wants to know the facts, the content, the substance, with little unnecessary ornamentation.

Beginning with Eusebius's *Ecclesiastical History*, our author has traveled through the centuries of Christian thought and reflection, stopping to examine and report on the lives and the spiritual insights of some of the giants of the Christian tradition. Saint Benedict, Saint John of the Cross, Saint Teresa of Ávila, Saint Thérèse of Lisieux and, in our own times, Jacques Maritain and C.S. Lewis, all are subjects of the inquiring mind and facile pen of our author.

When one contemplates personalities as different as Saint Benedict and Saint John of the Cross, or when one realizes how different are the worlds occupied by Saint Anselm and Saint Thérèse of Lisieux, one can easily be tempted to see these portraits as separate and independent vignettes. In many ways they are. Yet the more one reflects on the depths of the messages each of these

Christian giants has given us, the more one realizes the genius of Christianity that unites them with one another and with us in the ageless quest of seeking God through the person of his Son, Jesus Christ, in that mysterious communion which is ours in the Holy Spirit.

Dinesh D'Souza has served us all well by providing us with a sufficient taste of the spiritual thoughts of these great men and women so that we can be reassured about the richness of our tradition and be tempted to delve more deeply into their contributions to the Church. I hope that this book has a wide readership among the People of God because I am convinced that it can help to rejuvenate the lives of men and women who in our own days are seeking to bring forth the new as well as the old.

Bernard Cardinal Law
ARCHBISHOP OF BOSTON

O • N • E

eusebius's

ecclesiastical history

EUSEBIUS of Caesarea is regarded as the "Father of Church History," and with good reason. Without him, we would know very little about the origins of Christianity, the rapid spread of the early Church, the sanguinary persecutions and glorious martyrdoms, wild-eyed heresies and somber definitions on orthodoxy, all culminating in the ultimate triumph of Christian rule under Emperor Constantine in the fourth century after Christ. Eusebius brings his gifts as a historian, philosopher, theologian, and stylist to bear on his *Ecclesiastical History*, a work of breathtaking scope, spanning hundreds of years and many lands, including both Eusebius's own eyewitness testimony plus the reports and records of hundreds of other authorities. If not for Eusebius, a significant chapter of the most important development in the history of man — the birth and spread of Catholicism — would be lost.

The *Ecclesiastical History* is both an inspiring and surprising work. It uplifts because it revives that ancient and largely forgotten enthusiasm about the faith that the persecuted Christians embodied — according to Eusebius, they "found fulfillment in martyrdom." We

7

are accustomed in our own day to camps and gulags, yet there most people went to involuntary extermination; we realize that it must have taken a special courage for Christians, who could have repudiated God and saved their lives, to stand in immovable dignity as wild beasts pounced on them and tore them to pieces.

Conventional wisdom has it that the early Church was markedly different from our own: while today Catholicism is hierarchical, then it was democratic; while today it is doctrinal, then it was rooted in simple faith; while today it is bureaucratic, then it was primitive and spontaneous; while today there is ritual, then it was unceremonious. Eusebius punctures all these myths, and the credibility of his testimony is that he is not arguing against anyone's history; he is merely narrating what he saw and knew. We discover in Eusebius that the early Church bears close resemblance to that Catholicism to which we have become habituated. Almost at the outset we find a line of demarcation between clergy and laity. Right away we discover ecclesiastical distinctions between bishop, presbyter, and deacon. From the beginning we find the sacraments — ordination, baptism, and confirmation. Apostolic succession along with the authority

---

AUTHOR'S NOTE: The reader is advised to bear in mind that this book's aim is to acquaint him or her with the philosophies, thoughts, and insights of the personalities whose writings are the subject of this work, rather than to have the reader view it as a history book in the strict sense of the word. Hence, there may seem to be misspellings of proper names at times, but in actuality they are usually variants of the same name (for instance, Leibniz instead of Leibnitz in Chapter 3); the same goes for dates, place-names, and the like, the reason being that historians and other compilers of "facts" do not always agree on details.

of the Church of Rome is at once inaugurated and widely accepted. The problem of heresy, which we sometimes identify with later centuries, or even the Reformation, actually plagued the Church in the first century — Eusebius recounts some now-forgotten heresies, and others in which we find a familiar ring.

At first glance it appears that everybody in the fourth century was named Eusebius. We know of at least forty contemporaries who bore the same name. Our Eusebius, author of the *Ecclesiastical History*, was born in the limestone city of Caesarea near the coast of Palestine around the year A.D. 260. We don't know much about his life; it is clear that he was an intellectual prodigy, who had published several books by the time he was a young man. He studied briefly under the great Eastern philosopher Origen; later, when Origen's speculations came under attack, Eusebius would write a spirited *Defense of Origen*. Eusebius lived in an epoch of danger — not only were the Jews hostile to the burgeoning Christian faith but the Roman Empire felt threatened by its rapid spread. Not only did Christianity face persecution from without but it also suffered internal divisions. Eusebius was twice imprisoned for his Christian beliefs — once in 309 near Palestine, then in 311 in Egypt. Nevertheless he refused to renounce his faith and his dedication and writings brought him much acclaim. In 314 he was consecrated bishop of Caesarea, a position he occupied for the rest of his life.

His output was truly prodigious. He composed almost fifty books, several of them in ten or more volumes, often issued in new editions with revisions and updating. When you consider how few his resources were — no libraries, no telephones, no indexes, no pens, typewriters, personal computers, or copying machines — his phenomenal stamina (and that of his scribes, transcribing words on papyrus) becomes evident. Eusebius wrote commentaries on several books of the Old and New Testaments, an account of the lives of the early martyrs, a *Panegyric on Constantine*, and one book strangely titled *The Numerous Progeny of the Ancients*. Although of tolerant and even temperament, he also published criticisms of early heresies, such as those of Marcellus and the Manichees. In his masterpiece, the *Ecclesiastical History*, Eusebius seeks to do more than fulfill historical curiosity; he wants to reinforce the confidence and faith of succeeding generations, and to vindicate — in the fashion of Milton — the ways of God to men.

Edward Gibbon accuses Eusebius of adorning his *History* with tall tales and falsehood — "He indirectly confesses that he has related whatever might redound to the glory, and has suppressed all that could tend to the disgrace, of religion" — but scholarship has redeemed Eusebius of this charge. While his *History* is not free of error, the mistakes are understandable, even excusable, in view of the obstacles that confronted him as a historian; there is certainly no evidence of malice or deliberate distortion.

Eusebian miracles, which have been much scoffed at, are in most cases merely the infusion of supernatural meaning into natural events, such as when he claims that God penalized the Jews for their rejection of Christ, or avaricious bishops by depriving them of their ill-gotten gains. Sometimes Eusebius is himself ambivalent about a fantastic account he has heard; on one occasion he says, "I know full well that this will seem a delusion or a myth to those after us, but not to those for whom the event made the truth credible."

The *Ecclesiastical History* is not always easy reading. First of all, its topics are so diverse. Eusebius discusses everything from disputes over the order of compositions of the Gospels, to the question of which Apostles were married, to the controversy over the proper date for the celebration of Easter. These are not questions that excite the adrenaline today. Eusebius is also a great quoter and citer: he constantly invokes Scripture; Church Fathers such as Irenaeus and Clement; historians such as Josephus and Thucydides; philosophers such as Origen and Plato. Among the immense catalog of martyrs, Eusebius describes the ordeals of almost one hundred fifty; among the almost equally numerous heresies, Eusebius gives us no less than forty-seven. Nevertheless there is a grand momentum and sweep to Eusebius's narrative that overwhelms and transcends individual detail. There is no danger of Eusebius losing the reader who can distinguish the forest from the trees.

Eusebius begins at the very beginning, with an account of the fall of Adam and its consequence. "His descendants, who peopled all our world, showed themselves much worse than he, plunging into a beastly existence and a life not worth living. City and state, arts and sciences meant nothing to them; laws and statutes, morality and philosophy were not even names; they lived a nomadic life in the desert like wild and savage creatures; nature's gift of reasoning and the germs of thought and culture in the human soul were destroyed by the immensity of their deliberate wickedness. Unholy practices of every kind had taken complete possession of them, so that at one time they corrupted, at another they murdered each other, at yet another they became cannibals; they planned to fortify earth against heaven, and in the madness of a deranged mind prepared for war against the Ruler of all things Himself." This is both an allusion to literal events as well as a general backdrop to Eusebius's own theme: the struggle of the faith to survive in an environment hostile to the God of that faith.

Eusebius also relays, at the outset, God's dual strategy. At first, he says, "With continual famines and pestilences and again with wars and thunderbolts from the sky, God cut men off, making his punishments more and more drastic as if to check some terrible and well-nigh fatal sickness of the soul." But force was allied with goodness, justice with mercy. God also sent his Son, "the divine and heavenly Word of God," to become man and pay the penalty of sin. God is both the chastising father and the sacrificial brother. He permits horrible persecutions in order to give Christians opportunities for heroic martyrdom; then he avenges himself on the persecutors.

Occasionally in Eusebius one detects a note of glee when God gets even; here is his account of Herod's demise: "He had an overpowering desire for food, which it was impossible to satisfy, ulceration of the intestines with agonizing pains in the lower bowel, and a clammy transparent humor [a type of bodily fluid, according to the ancients] covering the feet. The abdomen was in the same miserable state. As for the genitals, mortification set in, breeding worms. He suffered in every part convulsions that were unbearably severe." Eusebius is by no means finished; he goes on to narrate how Herod went into a wild frenzy, ordering his own son and relatives executed, incarcerating his own eminent advisers, and attempting suicide to arrest his multiplying agonies. Such, Eusebius would have us know, was the fate of the man who put to death the firstborn of his state, in his attempt to destroy the Messiah who was Christ. Herod died in the year 4 B.C., in the reign of Augustus Caesar.

About Christ Eusebius gives us the fascinating anecdote of King Abgar of Mesopotamia, "who was dying from a terrible physical disorder which no human power could heal," so he sent word to Jesus about whom he had heard, requesting that Christ come and heal him. Eusebius gives us the actual text of Christ's reply: "I must complete all that I was sent to do here, and on completing it must at once be taken up to the One who sent me." Nevertheless Jesus sends a disciple, Thaddeus, in his place, and Thaddeus cures Abgar; as a result the whole nation of Edessa is converted to Christianity.

How did the Roman senate react to reports of Jesus' resurrection? Eusebius cites accounts that the event was widely discussed and debated in Palestine, and Pilate communicated what he knew about it to the emperor Tiberius, who submitted a report to the senate. But it was rejected, not on its merits but because of political and bureaucratic reasons, Eusebius writes. The senate vote, far from disturbing Eusebius, pleases him: "No human decision or commendation is required for the saving teaching of the divine message." He is alert, in other words, to the condescension of a group of mortals deigning to approve or ratify the resurrection.

The resurrection was undoubtedly the galvanizing event in Christianity. "At once, in accordance with the Scriptures, the voice of inspired evangelists and apostles went forth into all the earth, and their words to the ends of the world. In every town and village, like a well-filled threshing floor, churches shot up bursting with eager members."

Under Claudius and Nero, wars broke out between the Jews and the Romans, and famine ravaged the countryside. Eusebius limns the portrait of the learned Philo of Alexandria, defending the Jewish heritage before Roman senators, who responded with ignorant laughter and derision, kicking him out of the room. During one famine noted by Josephus, "all human feelings yielded to hunger, and decency was the first victim. Thus it was that wives robbed their husbands, children their fathers, and — most horrible of all — mothers their babes, snatching food out of their mouths." Eusebius, who does not believe in euphemism, gives a gory detailed account of Mary, daughter of Eleazar, who roasted and ate her child, then invited starving relatives and friends: "Help yourselves, I have had my share."

Among the many martyrdoms recounted by Eusebius, the most lengthy and powerful is the story of Polycarp of Smyrna. Saint Irenaeus tells us that the youthful Polycarp had been "instructed by the Apostles, and had familiar intercourse with many who had seen Christ." Thus he is a link joining the traditions of the earliest founders of Christianity with the new religion's theologians and canonists of the late second century. The Romans seized Polycarp in the year 155. He was brought into the arena of wild beasts but refused to submit to the roar of the crowd. So fearsome was the mob's appetite for blood, Eusebius reports, that other Christians broke down: "A man named Quintus, newly arrived from Phrygia, on seeing the beasts and the threatened torments gave up completely and threw away his salvation."

The Romans urged Polycarp to accept the total sovereignty and lordship of Caesar: "What harm is there in saying Lord Caesar? What harm is there in renouncing this God of yours?" Polycarp coolly replied, "For eighty-six years I have been his servant, and He has never done me wrong. How can I now blaspheme the King who saved me?" Polycarp was informed that if lions did not scare him he would be taunted with fire. "The fire you threaten burns for a time and is soon extinguished," Polycarp said, drawing himself to full height. "There is a fire you know nothing about — the fire of judgement to come, and of eternal punishment, a fire reserved for the ungodly." Then, Eusebius says, "The crowds rushed to collect logs and faggots from workshops and public baths." Polycarp was bound "like a noble ram" and set ablaze. But even as the wall of fire surrounded him, Eusebius says, "we were conscious of a wonderful fragrance, like a breath of frankincense," and thus was Polycarp's martyrdom accepted as an offering by God. Eusebius goes on and on about Polycarp, and no wonder. He was there, and the incident affected him deeply.

Another harrowing account is that of the martyr Blandina, distinguished by her stubborn refusal to be finished off, despite the variety and imagination of Roman punishment. At first she was beaten, raped, and tortured, to the point where her persecutors "were exhausted by their efforts and confessed themselves defeated — they could think of nothing else to do to her. Indeed they were amazed that she was still breathing, for her whole body was mangled and her wounds gaped." Nevertheless Blandina staunchly spoke the word of Christ. Finally, Eusebius reports, "she was dropped in a basket and thrown to a bull. Time after time the animal tossed her, but she was indifferent now to all that happened to her." She died in the knowledge that she would go straight to heaven, and even the heathen were amazed and "admitted they had never known a woman to suffer so much or so long."

A number of senior officials in the Roman administration and army converted to Catholicism; several were forced to choose between their rank and their religion.

Eusebius tells us about Marinus, who was promoted to one of the top posts in the militia. But when the Romans discovered he was a Christian they debarred him, giving him three hours to rethink his confession of Christianity. At the end, Marinus was summoned to the altar by the bishop of his diocese, who pointed to the Bible on the table and the sword at his side. Marinus would have to choose one, he said. Marinus unhesitatingly put his hand on the Bible. Then he went back to the court, where he was executed.

The persecutions reached their zenith around the time of Emperor Diocletian. In his first edict Diocletian mandated that all churches be destroyed, all worship cease, and the Scriptures be burned. A second edict commanded that clergy be imprisoned. A third directed that all clergy engage in pagan sacrifice on pain of torture. The fourth edict, issued in 304, extended the requirement of participation in pagan rites to laity as well. The rigor with which these directives were enforced varied according to the zeal and sadism of local officials administering the vast Roman empire.

During the great persecution which broke out in A.D. 303 and lasted about a decade, Eusebius tells us that "God's worshippers perished wholesale and in heaps, some butchered with the sword, others fulfilled by the fire; it is on record that with an inspired and mystical fervor men and women alike leapt on the pyre. A number of others were bound by the public executioners, dumped in small boats, and thrown into the depths of the sea." Among the animals used in the arenas were lions, panthers, bears, wild boars, and bulls goaded with red-hot irons. "You would see a youngster not yet twenty standing without fetters," Eusebius says, "spreading out his arms in the form of a cross, and with a mind unafraid and

16

unshakable, occupying himself in the most unhurried prayers to the Almighty, not budging in the least and not retreating from the spot where he stood, though bears and panthers breathing fury attacked his flesh." In Thebes Christians were tied to tightly-drawn boughs of trees that were then released, tearing their limbs apart. So arduous was all this that it took its toll on executioners, who, Eusebius tells us, had to be periodically relieved and replaced. For the most refractory Christians, ingenuities of punishment were greatly valued by the Romans — whether it was pointed reeds driven into the fingers, or boiling soot poured over the body, these innovations were developed "as if they were taking part in a prize competition, trying their hardest to put each other in the shade."

Fortunately, Eusebius says, the persecutor sometimes paid for his crimes. One hapless fellow "was pursued by a divinely ordained punishment, which began with his flesh and went on into his soul. Without warning suppurative inflammation broke out round the middle of his genitals, then a deep-seated fistular ulcer. These ate their way incurably into his bowels. From them came a teeming indescribable mass of worms, and a sickening smell was given off, for the whole of his hulking body, thanks to overeating, had been transformed into a huge lump of flabby fat, which then decomposed and presented those who came near with a revolting and horrifying sight." Eusebius tops this off with a couple of quotations from Scripture to the effect that he who pits himself against the Lord comes to a bad end.

One of the anomalies of history is that even dignified and enlightened Roman emperors, such as Marcus Aurelius and Trajan, did not abstain from persecuting Christians. They were possessed of every human virtue, it appears, yet they could not detect in the new faith the light of the divine. It is true that Trajan, in a hint of humanitarianism, wrote a letter to Pliny the Younger advising that Christians not be pursued for harassment, although if cases turned up they were of course to be prosecuted.

Eusebius is devastating in refuting those apologists for the Roman empire who are enthusiastic in their praise for rulers who moderated persecution and harassment of Christians. Here is an edict of Maximin: "It is necessary for you, noble and law-abiding judges, to exercise merciful and humane conduct in your dealings with the Christians. Therefore the benefit of our humane imperial authority is to be extended to all, and the death penalty is not to be imposed on the Christians. The penalty instead for those Christians who refuse to recant is the gouging out of an eye or the maiming of a leg. This lighter punishment will demonstrate our imperial compassion." Allowing an exception to this rule, Maximin ordered Agapius the Christian thrown to the beasts of Caesarea as part of his birthday celebration in the autumn of A.D. 307. It is ironic that Renaissance defenders of these Roman authoritarians are now regarded as the founders of modern humanism.

Because of the unquestioned status of ecclesiastical authorities, Eusebius is particularly keen to hold them to the higher standards to which they are called; thus he is boldly critical of priests and bishops who failed to lead in time of duress. For those who think that Church hierarchy began with the Council of Trent or later, the writings of early Church historians and Church Fathers will come as a surprise. Here, for instance, is Ignatius of Antioch: "Abjure all factions, for they are the beginning of evil. Follow your bishop, every one of you, as obediently as Jesus Christ followed the Father. Obey your clergy too, as you would the Apostles. The sole Eucharist you should consider valid is one that is celebrated by the bishop or one authorized by him." The argument of Ignatius and Eusebius is that if we want to be true to Christ, whom we cannot see, we should follow his earthly representative, the bishop, whom we can see. Eusebius chastises clergy who, during persecution, "shamefully hid themselves here and there while others were ignominiously captured." He denounces "those supposed to be our shepherds, casting aside the sanctions of the fear of God, inflamed by contentions with one another . . . claiming primacies as if they were tyrant's spoils."

Besides persecutions, and the courage and cowardice they engendered, the other grand theme in Eusebius's *Ecclesiastical History* is that of heresy. This is a theme closer to us in the West today. Certainly persecution of Christianity is not halted, but it is predominantly concentrated in the Eastern Communist bloc. In the West, Christianity is more ignored than punished; as Thomas Carlyle put it some time ago, "If Jesus Christ were alive today, we would not crucify him. We would invite him to dinner, listen to what he had to say, and then make fun of it." Contemporary persecution, however, has helped give unity and purpose to churches in Poland and other countries. In the West, by contrast, Christianity is divided — even undermined — from within itself. As a recent pope comments, the smoke of Satan is now inside the Church. Thus, it is with particular interest that we consider what Eusebius has to say about those who broke ranks with Catholicism.

Some readers will be shocked to discover that heresy was virtually coexistent with the Church's founding; Eusebius gives us the case of the infamous Gnostic, Simon the Magus, during the first ten years of Catholicism. He was "the prime author of every heresy," Eusebius says, with some overstatement. Eusebius is severe on those who "pretend to accept the sober Christian philosophy" while remaining in fact "devoted as ever to the idolatrous superstition from which they claimed to have escaped." They are "brim full of frenzy and lunacy." Even firmly convinced dissidents who went to martyrdom for their beliefs do not impress Eusebius; he attributes their strength to the power of magic and demonic spirits. Eusebius expresses satisfaction that Simon could not gain the following to establish an independent base of power; rather his rebellion arose, was refuted, and subsided.

Not so with other heresies, which gained converts and caused lasting dissension and pain to the faith. There was Menander, who somehow persuaded a number of Christians that they would not die — an understandably appealing delusion but presumably one that could be shown to be empirically false. The Ebionites, Eusebius says, regarded Christ as a righteous but quite ordinary man, "the child of a normal union between a man and Mary." The fact that Eusebius casually throws this in tells us something important — the doctrine of the Virgin Birth of Christ was widely accepted during the earliest days of the Church; it was not, as some now imply, a later Catholic invention. The heretic Cerinthus announced that the promised kingdom of Christ would not be an imaginary heaven but here on earth; he promised fantastic carnality and bacchanalia, complete with a thousand-year period given to wedding festivities. A related heresy came from one Nicolaus, who believed jealousy to be the one great human evil; to prove that he was not given to it, he invited early Christians to have sex with his wife. If he wanted perverse pleasures or illegitimate babies he didn't get them, however; the Christians refused, and Nicolaus was ostracized. Basilides the heretic came up with his own list of prophets, including Barcabbas and Barcoph, heretofore unknown. He also declared that there was no problem if Christians renounced the faith in times of persecution, as long as they took it up again. To prove his sincerity Basilides maintained a five-year period of silence and forced his followers to do the same — fortunately little was heard from them subsequently. Then there was Tatian, a disciple of Justin Martyr who went astray after Justin's death; Tatian repudiated marriage as being depravity and fornication; he also denied that it was possible for Adam to be saved. Novatus, several years later, proclaimed that Christians who had shown cowardice during the height of the Roman persecutions were damned whether they repented or not; he was unanimously condemned by an early Church council in Rome.

The one heresy that Eusebius was himself initially sympathetic toward was a particularly popular and dangerous one: Arianism, which denied the Trinity and the divinity of Christ. The argument of Arius was that God the Father was the uncreated being, the Unoriginate, as he put it. Thus it was ludicrous to maintain that Christ, his Son, was Unoriginate as well — rather Christ was a created being who derived from God the Father. The brilliant theologian Origen argued that Christ and the Holy Spirit "participated," in a Neoplatonic fashion, in the perfect divinity of God the Father. But Origen did not put Christ and the Holy Spirit on coequal terms with the Father. Eusebius, a student of Origen, staunchly defended the master.

Origen was admittedly an odd character. In one of

his fundamentalist moments he took literally the words of Matthew 19:12 — ". . . there are eunuchs who have made themselves eunuchs for the sake of the kingdom of heaven" — and castrated himself. Nevertheless Origen's clarity and effulgence of thought continued to have a strong sway in the Church even though specific errors into which he lapsed were later condemned. Of Origen it should be said that he continually sought orthodoxy and fidelity to Catholic teaching, which is more than can be said of Arius, who mounted direct artillery against the see of Rome. Eusebius came to appreciate the threat that Arian disunity posed to the Church, and he voted against Arius at the Council of Nicaea where, with the help of Saint Athanasius, the Trinity was defined as three coequal persons in one God.

Eusebius is clearly no friend of heresy. With pride he quotes the time that the martyr Polycarp came face-to-face with the dissenter Marcion. "Don't you recognize me?" Marcion inquired. "I do indeed," Polycarp replied. "I recognize the firstborn of Satan." Eusebius tells us the story of Saint John who, upon hearing that the heretic Cerinthus was inside, made a hasty exit from the public baths so as not to allow himself to be contaminated. Eusebius argues that the devil works through heresy to darken "the radiance of the universal and only true church" that "always holds the same doctrines in the same way." Ecumenism was not particularly popular in Eusebius's day. In the *Ecclesiastical History* he approvingly notes, "Wisely careful were the apostles and their disciples to avoid even exchanging words with falsifiers of truth."

At the same time Eusebius exhibits a spirit of openness to fair and well-intentioned debate within the Church. We can argue about when and how to observe fasts before Easter, he says, and still remain good Christians, and friends. "The divergency in the fast emphasizes the unanimity of our faith." Eusebius gives an example of true dialogue that results not in polarization and recrimination but a deeper understanding of the truth: "I called a meeting of the presbyters and teachers of the village congregations, with any laymen who wished to attend, and urged them to thrash out the question in public. So they brought me this book as positive and irrefutable proof, and I sat with them for three days on end from dawn to dusk, criticizing its contents point by point. In the process I was immensely impressed by the essential soundness, complete sincerity, logical grasp, and mental clarity shown by these good people, as we methodically and good-temperedly dealt with questions, objections and points of agreement. We refused to cling with pig-headed determination to opinions once held even if proven wrong. There was no shirking of difficulties, but to the limit of our powers we tried to grapple with the problems and master them; nor were we too proud, if worsted in argument, to abandon our position and admit defeat; conscientiously, honestly, and with simple-minded trust in God, we accepted the conclusions to be drawn from the proofs and teachings of Holy Writ. In the end, the author and originator of this doctrine, Coracion by name, in the hearing of all present, assured and promised us that for the future he would not adhere to it, argue about it, mention it, or teach it, as he was completely convinced of the arguments on the other side."

The *Ecclesiastical History* ends with the ascent of Emperor Constantine, a convert to Christianity, to the throne. Eusebius is jubilant about it, and extremely severe on Licinius, an associate of Constantine who was hostile to Catholicism. Eusebius accuses him of expelling

Christians from the ranks of government, even though they were for the first time being allowed to hold these posts. He faults Licinius for harassing bishops, even putting some to death, and throwing one poor fellow from a church roof. Finally Licinius is faulted for "using countless married women and unwedded girls to satisfy his own unbridled lust, the besotted old dotard." Happily Licinius is defeated at Chrysopolis in A.D. 324 and Constantine emerges as sole ruler.

Immediately Constantine removed the ban on Christianity, which had been the *raison d'être* for the earlier persecutions. Christianity began to enjoy new respectability; gradually it would become the mainstream. The Edict of Milan, signed by Constantine, declared that "Christians and non-Christians alike should be allowed to keep the faith of their own religious beliefs and worship." Eusebius's enthusiasm about Constantine was reciprocated when the emperor asked Eusebius to deliver the opening address at the Nicaean Council, which he chaired. Eusebius's last years, before his death in A.D. 340, were restful and contented ones; he knew that the once-embattled faith was entering a new era. What he did not know was that soon Christianity would become the accepted state religion in the Holy Roman Empire; later in the fourth century, Theodosius would proclaim that nonbelievers should be deprived of all rights to hold jobs. "It is sufficient for the atheist that he has a right to exist." Eusebius also did not know that Christianity would spread its influence across the globe, enduring and flourishing for over a millennium, ready to take on challenges of equal proportions to the one it encountered in its embryonic stage.

T • W • O

benedict's

monastic rule

S ELDOM has a document more closely governed the lives of more people over a longer period of time than the famous *Rule* of Saint Benedict. Written in the sixth century against the panoramic backdrop of the fall of Roman civilization to the barbarian invaders, the *Rule* acquired a gradual hold on the imagination of the developing Christian culture. It remained the controlling principle of the monastery tradition for almost a thousand years. Even today the legacy of Benedict lives on through the Benedictine order, even though the precepts of the *Rule* have been diluted to the point where it is more important historically and intellectually than practically.

Benedict's life is known to us largely through the biography written shortly after his death by Gregory the Great, the first Benedictine pope. We learn that Benedict was born in the region of Nursia, north of Rome, around A.D. 480. His early religious conversion inspired him to forsake worldly pleasures and join an ascetic order pledged to a three-year vow of silence. Then Benedict migrated to another order of monks, but found them to be "false monks," unfaithful to the Gospel. Benedict moved on to establish two famous houses, one at Monte Cassino on the way to Naples, another at Terracina. Soon these communities would be razed by the invading Lombards, but Benedict's recruits and disciples would furtively carry his written legacy to other monasteries; thus, in ever widening circles, Benedict's *Rule* would govern the institutions and hearts of generations of men and women devoted to the contemplative life.

Gregory the Great portrays Benedict as a solitary genius, moved by divine epiphany to invent his formula for monastic organization, but twentieth-century scholarship suggests that Benedict owes a good deal of his proposals to previous monastic "rules," in particular the *Regula Magistri*, composed by an unknown author, probably in the early sixth century. Thus today we are less likely to view Benedict as the great composer and more as the great synthesizer and the great teacher, absorbing diverse ideas from diverse cultures, integrating them into a concise and practical vision, then transmitting them in a form designed to endure vicissitudes of fate and time. "The *Rule* was appreciated not because it was original, but because it was traditional," notes Timothy Fry, O.S.B., in a recent appraisal. Precisely for this reason, it is important to view the *Rule* in the context of previous and subsequent Christian history; it grew out of that environment and decisively shaped it for the future.

Monasticism did not originate in Benedict's time; it has roots in the early Christian Church. The Bible itself emphasizes self-denial in its exaltation of concepts such as virginity and celibacy — important ingredients of the monastic tradition. Nevertheless early Christian asceticism should be distinguished from monasticism. The first- and second-century ascetics lived abstemiously in the midst of society; monasticism, by contrast, was characterized by a deliberate withdrawal from society and the creation of a separate, wholly independent, monastic culture dedicated to communal lifelong worship of Christ.

Monasticism of this sort was unknown to Eusebius; because he did not mention it in his *Ecclesiastical History*, we can plausibly surmise that it was not widespread. It grew rapidly, though, and by the end of the fourth century it was everywhere, luring priests and laity, young men and old. Some monasteries and abbots exercised such a magnetic attraction that mothers had to hide their children from exposure if they didn't want to give them up to a life of fasting, vegetarianism, prayer, and work in the fields.

Ironically Christians withdrew from secular society into monasteries just around the time that Western civilization succumbed to Christian conversion. Previously Christians formed secret enclaves to elude the terrible persecutions of Nero and Diocletian, but after Constantine removed the ban against Christianity, and the Edict of Milan legitimized the new faith, Christianity quickly moved into the mainstream; indeed it became the state religion and the dominant influence in Western culture. Exactly for this reason, though, many who were born into the faith, or converted to it, began to sense the corruptions and compromises that came with secular power. They felt the need to truncate themselves from society, and retreat either into individual nomadic existence — like Christ in the desert — or into cenobitic life, where communities of monks would spend the entire day in meditation upon, and service to, Christ.

Monasticism probably began in the Eastern church, where its outstanding figure was Saint Basil (circa 330-379). Even early on, asceticism began to develop problems of extremism; Basil helped assemble a regional council at Gangres to condemn monks who rejected marriage as unholy and taught that married couples could never reach heaven. A "moderate" wing of this group did not deny salvation to the wedded, but allowed them to get off with an extended stint in purgatory. Basil also rejected the minute regulation of items of clothing and food. He emphasized that the monastic life was nothing more than the Christian life lived seriously. Basil did not compose a "rule" for monasteries because he believed that they should be entirely based on the Christian rule of Scripture. In particular, he believed that the commandment to love God and our neighbor, if followed and given practical realization, would address all situations. Partly through Basil's influence, monasticism consolidated itself in Asia Minor and Egypt.

A good bit of Western monasticism was imported from the East, but some of it had indigenous roots. In Italy Saint Ambrose, upon being named bishop of Milan in 374, gave up his lavish estates and adopted the ascetic life; he founded a monastery at Milan, where men were sworn to celibacy and virgins consecrated to lives of chaste devotion to God. Saint Jerome and a female disciple named Paula traveled to the Holy Land where they founded two monasteries, one for men and one for women. Jerome, having translated the Old Testament from Hebrew to Latin and written several commentaries on the Scriptures, helped inaugurate a strong habit of biblical study in these seminaries. The Bethlehem monasteries would make valuable contributions to biblical scholarship in subsequent years. In Gaul Saint Martin of Tours, formerly a military man and part-time exorcist, renounced his arms and propagated monasticism, toppling pagan shrines and setting up monasteries in their place. When he died, it is said that two thousand monks attended his funeral, and Saint Benedict dedicated one of the shrines at his own monastery at Monte Cassino to the beloved and revered Martin. There was the intellectual influence of John Cassian, who hailed from a monastery at Marseilles. He was familiar both with the Eastern and Western monastic traditions, as they evolved, and reconciled their principles and practices in his *Institutes* — cited and recommended in Benedict's *Rule* because of its wide usage of practical wisdom.

Perhaps the most influential monastic rule before that of Benedict was the Rule of Saint Augustine. Great emphasis is laid there on equality of social condition. Whatever the standing in the world of people before they enter the monastery, Augustine maintains, once inside they are all equal. We will see that Benedict draws on the notion of classlessness that Augustine popularized. One should not believe that there are no distinctions in the monastery — that would be unusual in a hierarchical church; rather, one should realize that distinctions are based on divine authority, not human inheritance or human custom.

Around the time of Benedict's *Rule*, the multicolored currents of heresy swirled around both Eastern and Western churches. In the East, Nestorianism, which denied the divinity of Christ, enjoyed wide appeal even after it was condemned by the Council of Ephesus in 431. Strangely, another prevalent Eastern heresy was Monophysitism, which accepted Christ's divinity but rejected his humanity — holding that Christ merely appeared to be human, although that appearance was illusory. The West, in turn, was beleaguered by the Pelagian heresy, which emphasized free will to the point of denying original sin or the need for divine grace; this error was a special temptation to monks because, having made great personal sacrifices to live a life patterned on the Gospel, they were disposed to attribute their redemption to their own will and works. Perhaps the most popular and dangerous of all heresies was Arianism — involving the denial of the Trinity — which was attractive to barbarian rulers who sacked Rome. Benedict's *Rule*, by setting parameters both for prayer and practice, attempts to keep Christian monasteries free from the offending influences of heresy and rebellion.

The *Rule* is a handbook or guide that advises Christians on how to establish and live the monastic life. In contrast to previous rules, it is remarkably laconic and cogent. It resists the tendency to legislate on all questions or control the minutiae of people's lives. It is supple and allows for varied adaptation to changing circumstances. At the same time it is firm in its articulation of biblical precepts, allowing concessions with visible reluctance, and in several cases recommending stern punishments. Finally the *Rule* is intellectually sweeping, not only on its coverage of all aspects of monastic life, but also in its usage of ideas and practices from monasteries of Gaul, Africa, Egypt, Rome, and Naples. These heterogeneous influences are united and compressed into a document of striking clarity and integrity.

Gregory the Great, in his life of Benedict, tells us that from his youth Benedict was captivated by the still-luminous glory of old Rome. It took him three years of silent prayer at Subiaco before his conversion to the monastic life was complete. During that time a friendly monk named Romanus brought him food, which he would let down over a cliff with a long rope, fastened with a bell to alert Benedict in his cave. Jealous monks in Subiaco tried to corrupt Benedict by sending him depraved women; eventually Benedict simply packed up his belongings and, at the age of fifty, made his way south to the place where he would establish his first monastery, Monte Cassino.

"The monastery should, if possible, be so arranged that all necessary things, such as water, mill, garden and various workshops may be within the enclosure, so that the monks will not be compelled to wander outside it, for this is altogether expedient for their souls." Thus writes Benedict in his *Rule*, and Monte Cassino was modeled to be a self-sufficient enclave of Christian faith and practice.

Written in colloquial Latin, the *Rule* makes no pretension to greatness. It is a "little rule for beginners," Benedict submits, in a tone of humility he will recommend for all monks. The *Rule* emphasizes a lay apostolate. Perhaps surprising to many of us today, most monks in those times were not clergy; indeed Benedict recommends that priests not be easily allowed to join monasteries, and if they do their main function is to give the sacraments to the lay monks. The *Rule* also stresses communal life and worship — Benedict argues that individual isolation from society does not cultivate virtues of obedience, humility, charity toward others, and sharing of possessions, which the Bible mandates. Perhaps eventually, Benedict believes, when monks transform their corrupt human dispositions, they will be eligible and ready for a life of individual contemplation, cut off not just from society, but also from other Christians, interacting only with the God in the heavens. But Benedict knows it is a long way from an impetuous young convert to the ash and snows of Saint Bernard.

The *Rule* follows a consistent pattern — on each subject the spiritual principles are first enunciated, then their practical consequences are spelled out in detail.

The *Rule* is peppered with biblical quotations that sometimes merge with Benedict's prose and have to be excavated from it. The *Rule* covers virtually every dimension of the life of a monk, from the liturgical code, to disciplinary proceedings, to acceptance and rejection of new members, to prayer life, to the selection of the abbot, the prior, and even the monastery porter.

The *Rule* specifies that it should not be easy to be admitted to the monastery; that way, only the spiritually serious will enter. When a new applicant knocks on the door, for instance, Benedict suggests that he be left outside, unanswered and unattended for a while. "If such a one, therefore, perseveres in his knocking, and if it be seen after four or five days that he bears patiently the difficulty of admission and persists in his petition, then let admittance be granted to him." But for a whole year he should be under the direct care and supervision of an appointed senior monk, who should read to him aloud three times the *Rule*, and also extract written vows of conversion of life and total obedience. A varied form of this Benedictine initiation continues in the Catholic order bearing the saint's name to this day.

"We intend to establish a school for the Lord's service," Benedict proclaims at the outset. "In drawing up its regulations, we hope to set down nothing harsh, nothing burdensome. The good of all concerned, however, may prompt us to a little strictness in order to amend faults and to safeguard love." At once the firmness and yet moderation of the *Rule* shines through. Benedict is encouraging — "Do not be daunted immediately by fear and run away from the road that leads to salvation, even though it is bound to be narrow" — and at the same time candid: "We shall through patience share in the sufferings of Christ that we may deserve to share in his kingdom."

Not all monks, Benedict warns, are worthy of the name. Probably in reference to his own experience with "false monks," he refers obliquely to monks who are "always on the move, never settling down, slaves to their own wills and gross appetites." Other monks, though settled in houses, are equally wayward in a spiritual sense. "Their law is what they like to do, whatever strikes their fancy. Anything they believe in and choose, they call holy; anything they dislike, they consider forbidden." Right away Benedict is calling for order and authority to arbitrate individual differences and whims; he rejects "anything goes" Christianity. Benedict, however, does not want to waste time on deviant monks. "It is better to keep silent than to speak of these and their disgraceful way of life." He moves on to the shape of monastic life, not as it unfortunately is in some places, but as it should be in all.

The emphasis in the Benedictine monastery is on prayer and work. Here is a suggested schedule: the monks rise at 2:00 A.M. and say Vigils or the night office. Then follows an hour's meditation or reading. Lauds are said at 4:30 or early dawn, Prime at sunrise around six, and reading fills the time until Terce at nine o'clock. Then come six or seven hours of work in the fields, with Sext said during the noon interval. After Vespers at 4:30, the only meal of the day ends with Compline at dusk, 6:00 P.M. Mass is said on Sundays and holy days, and sins are confessed publicly to other monks if they are public sins, privately to the abbot if they are private sins that do not injure others.

Work and prayer are treated by Benedict as extensions of the same Christian devotion. Work is a form of prayer, and (certainly with the schedule Benedict outlines) prayer can be hard work. The purpose of both is to glorify God, dignify the individual, and bring shared blessings upon the community of monks. Benedict communicates a powerful vision of human dignity and spiritual unity, which has continued to underlie Catholic proclamations on the nature of work and labor. Benedict believed that it was the repetition of prayers and labors that would confer the habits of sanctity on the monk. That is why he emphasized physical work over intellectual effort. Benedict's Monte Cassino model was in contrast to that established by his rough contemporary, Cassiodorous, whose monastery at Vivarium exalted mental labor as the chief enterprise for the monks. Cassiodorus's model did not long survive, while Benedict's model took deeper and deeper root in the soil of Christian Europe.

Describing the organizational structure of monasteries, Benedict first defines the role of the head of the house, the abbot. Benedict is emphatic on one point — the abbot must be in absolute control over the goings-on at his monastery. Indeed the abbot holds the place of Christ, is addressed by a title of God ("abba," or father); thus he must be unquestioningly revered and obeyed. All the rules outlined in subsequent chapters of the document are subject to the discretion of the abbot, who must adapt life in the monastery to the needs and conditions he is faced with.

"In the monastery no one is to follow his own heart's desire, nor shall anyone presume to contend with his abbot defiantly, inside or outside the monastery," Benedict writes. During discussions, he adds, "The brothers are to express their opinions with all humility and not presume to defend their views obstinately. The decisions are the abbot's to make, so that when he has determined what is prudent, all must obey."

Yet Benedict realizes that with such power comes enormous responsibility. He firmly details the obligations the abbot faces. "The abbot must never teach or decree or command anything that deviates from the Lord's instruction." He must be immersed in Scripture and derive his orders from it. Further, "he must point to all that is good and holy by example as well as words . . . if he teaches that something is not to be done, then neither must he do it." The abbot should "avoid all favoritism . . . he is to show equal love to everyone and apply the same discipline to all." Yet Benedict is no radical egalitarian; he favors "distinctions according to merit" and gives the abbot "discretion to change anyone's rank as he sees fit or justice demands." Overall the abbot shoulders a heavy burden — he is nothing less than the good shepherd and "he will bear the blame where the sheep have yielded no profit," that is, he is ultimately accountable for the supernatural welfare of his flock.

Next Benedict proceeds to outline desirable conduct for the average monk. He is to "listen readily to holy reading," "every day with tears and sighs to confess past sins to God in prayer," and "change from evil ways in the future." Further Benedict advises, "Obey the orders of the abbot unreservedly, even if his own conduct — God forbid — be at odds with what he says." "Do not aspire to be called holy before you really are, but first be holy that you may more truly be called so." "If you have a dispute with someone, resolve to make peace with him before the sun goes down." "Be aware that God's gaze is upon you, wherever you are." Finally, "Never lose hope in God's mercy." We soon realize that many of these rules are not uniquely monastic; they apply, with equal relevance, to our own lives. Benedict calls them "the tools of the spiritual craft."

Each of Benedict's prohibitions and exhortations is spelled out in some detail. For instance, twelve objects, or goals, are described to justify the practice of humility. One is that "a man loves not his own will nor takes any pleasure in the satisfaction of his desires." He obeys all legitimate authority, so that "even under difficult, unfavorable or unjust conditions, his heart quietly embraces suffering." Humility is connected with the sacrament of confession: "A man does not conceal from his abbot any sinful thoughts entering his heart, or any wrongs committed in secret, but rather confesses them humbly." Monks should be content with "the lowest and most menial treatment, like that of a worthless workman." Humility entails a very different demeanor. "Whether he stands, walks or sits, the monk's head must be bowed and his eyes cast down"; Benedict compares the monk to the simple publican in the Gospel story. Finally "humility means that a monk should control his tongue and not speak unless asked a question." Above all, because this is unbecoming to his vocation, "a monk should not engage in boisterous laughter."

Slowly, Benedict says, these virtues, once acquired through hard striving and heavy discipline, become natural to the monk. "He will now begin to observe without effort, through habit, no longer out of fear of hell but of love of God." Now the rewards will begin to accrue to him. "After ascending all these steps of humility, the monk will arrive at that perfect love of God which casts out all tribulation."

The malleability and understanding of human frailty that characterizes the Benedictine *Rule* come through again and again. In describing the procedures for prayer on the Sabbath Benedict observes, "These arrangements for Sunday vigils should be followed at all times, summer and winter, unless — God forbid — the monks happen to arise too late. In that case the readings or responsories will have to be shortened." After ordering the psalms for weekly recitation Benedict adds, "If anyone finds this distribution of the psalms unsatisfactory, he should arrange whatever he judges better, provided that the full complement of one hundred and fifty psalms is by all means carefully maintained each week, and that the series begins anew each Sunday at vigils." Benedict is willing to make exceptions regarding the question of diet: "With respect to the very young and old, their lack of strength must always be taken into account. They should certainly be required to follow the strictness of the rule with regard to food, but should be treated kindly consideration and allowed to eat before regular hours." Despite its stern protocols, Benedict's *Rule* never fails to exude a warm humanity.

Moderation is even touched upon with a bit of light humor. "We do indeed read," Benedict says, referring to a manual for Eastern monks, "that wine is no drink for monks, but since nowadays monks cannot possibly be persuaded of this, let us agree that we drink temperately and not to satiety." What follows is provision for a daily measure of wine.

Here is Benedict on the sleeping arrangements for monks: "They sleep clothed, and girded with belts and cords, but they should remove their knives, lest they accidentally cut themselves in their sleep. . . . Monks are to sleep in separate beds at all times. . . . The younger brothers should not have their beds next to each other, but interspersed among the seniors. On arising for the work of God, they will quietly encourage each other, for the sleepy like to make excuses." Each sentence, if we think about it, represents practical and commonsense instruction, developed out of an understanding of human nature and especially temptation.

Benedict is fairly specific with regard to food and drink, although he allows that it should vary according to climate and terrain. In general "it is enough to provide all the tables with two kinds of cooked food, because in this way, the person [who] may not be able to eat one kind . . . [may] partake of another." Bread should be broken and shared in biblical fashion, and some of it saved over from lunch for supper. "Should it happen that work is heavier than usual, the abbot may decide to grant something additional, provided that overindulgence is avoided, lest a monk experience indigestion." Nothing, Benedict adds, "is so inconsistent with the life of a Christian."

Benedict counsels monks not to engage in excessive self-mortification, a rule he enforced in his own tenure as abbot. In Gregory's biography we read about Martin the hermit who lived in a cave on a mountainside not far from Monte Cassino. In order to demonstrate his spiritual seriousness, Martin apparently fastened himself to the rocky edge of his cave with an iron chain. When Benedict learned of this he sent Martin a message telling him, "If thou art a servant of God, let no chain of iron hold thee, but the chain of Christ." Gregory tells us that right away the hermit dispensed with the chain, and since then exhibited his fidelity to God through love and works of charity.

Throughout the *Rule* the focus is on simplicity and regularity of conduct. For instance, on hearing the dinner bell, "the monk will immediately set aside what he has in his hand and go with the utmost speed." No dawdling, in other words. Yet "he should move with gravity and without giving occasion for frivolity." No sprinting is permitted either. If a monk is late to choir, "he must take the last place of all, or the place set apart by the abbot for such offenders." Monks late to meals should be reproved the first time, asked to eat alone the second time, and deprived of wine thereafter until amends are made. "Should anyone make a mistake in a psalm, responsory, refrain or reading, he must make satisfaction there before all," Benedict writes. "Children, however, are to be whipped for such a fault."

Occasionally the *Rule* appears unduly Draconian. "In no circumstances is a monk allowed, unless the abbot says he may, to exchange letters, blessed tokens or small gifts of any kind, with his parents or anyone else, or with a fellow monk. He must not presume to accept gifts sent him even by his parents without previously telling the abbot." Partly this is because of Benedict's firm reading of the injunction in the Acts of the Apostles to hold possessions in common. The *Rule* severely castigates the ownership of private property. "This evil practice must be uprooted and removed from the monastery." Monks cannot hope to own goods, Benedict says, which should not surprise, since "monks may not have free disposal even of their own bodies and wills." All must be submitted to the abbot for prudent use and distribution according to need.

Gregory tells us of the time that one of the monks under Benedict's care was presented with some handkerchiefs by nuns who were particularly enchanted by one of his sermons. When he happily returned to the seminary, though, Benedict rebuked him: "How has evil entered into your bosom?" The monk was astonished, not even aware of what Benedict was complaining. "Am I not aware that you took the handkerchief from God's handmaids and put them in your bosom?" Benedict asked. The monk immediately fell at his feet, cast away the handkerchiefs, and asked forgiveness.

Fairly surprising, some even say revolutionary, is Benedict's rule for the election of abbots — "the guiding principles should always be [that] the man placed in office be the one elected either by the whole community acting unanimously in the fear of God, or by part of the community, no matter how small, which possesses sounder judgement." Here is the nucleus for democratic institutions in the monastic system, and for meritocracy, too: "Goodness of life and wisdom in teaching must be the criteria for choosing the one to be made abbot, even if he is the last in community rank."

Benedict appears hostile to the system of naming priors at monasteries and giving them near-equal authority to the abbot. He understands that dual power-sharing is a recipe for "envy, quarrels, slander, rivalry, factions and disorders of every kind," resulting in "the inevitable endangering of the souls of both abbot and prior." For the sake of both order and peace, Benedict urges, it is best for the abbot to make all decisions and the prior — if there is a prior — to be subordinate to him.

The *Rule* includes a pleasant and intriguing section on the monastery porter: "At the door of the monastery, place a sensible old man who knows how to take a message and deliver a reply, and whose age keeps him from roaming about. . . . As soon as anyone knocks, or a poor man calls out, the porter replies, 'Thanks be to God,' and then, with all the gentleness that comes from the fear of God, he provides a prompt answer with the warmth of love."

Finally there is the unpleasant business of excommunication and total severance, which Benedict deals with gravely but compassionately. He says that if repeated offenses of pride, disobedience, or other grave sins occur, first the monk should be warned privately by the seniors. "If he does not amend, he should be rebuked publicly in the presence of everyone." If that fails, "let him be excommunicated provided he understands the nature of his punishment. If however, he lacks understanding, let him undergo corporal punishment." Generally Benedict endorses the principle that "there ought to be due proportion between the seriousness of a fault and the measure of discipline."

Even excommunication, however, does not end the matter. Souls are not to be easily abandoned. "The abbot must exercise the utmost care and concern for wayward brothers, because it is not the healthy who need a physician, but the sick. Therefore, he ought to use every skill of a wise physician." Benedict even hints that while publicly condemning the excommunicated brother, the abbot may "under the cloak of secrecy, support him and urge him to be humble as a way of making satisfaction" and eventually restitution. "It is the responsibility of the abbot . . . not to lose any sheep entrusted to him," Benedict warns. "He is to imitate the example of the Good Shepherd who left the ninety-nine sheep in the mountains and went in search of the one that strayed." Benedict goes on to detail procedures for readmission after excommunication or expulsion.

Just as the *Rule* appears to be gaining momentum, cantering along in its treatment of one subject and the next, it abruptly comes to a halt. Benedict informs us that his rules are "only the beginning to perfection." He directs Christians to Scripture, to the writings of the Church Fathers, to commentaries. "Are you hastening toward your heavenly home?" Benedict asks. "Then, with Christ's help, keep this little rule. . . . After that,

41

you can set out for loftier summits of the teaching and virtues mentioned above, and under God's protection you will reach them. Amen.''

No wonder that this coruscating little book, this gem of advice and practical wisdom, endured for a millennium. Cardinal Newman writes of the spirit of Benedictinism: "The new world which he helped to create was a growth rather than a structure. Silent men were observed around the country, or discovered in the forest, digging, clearing, and building; and other silent men, not seen, were sitting in the cold cloister, tiring their eyes, and keeping their attention on the stretch, while they painfully copied and re-copied manuscripts which they had saved. There was no one that contended or cried out, or drew attention to what was going on; but by degrees the woody swamp became a hermitage, a religious house, a farm, an abbey, a village, a seminary, a school of learning, and a city.'' Thus were the foundations laid for medieval Christian Europe.

The *Rule* enjoyed a fitful and nomadic life in its early years. Written solely for Benedict's monastery at Monte Cassino, there is no record that it was followed elsewhere during Benedict's time. But when Monte Cassino fell in the late sixth century, the monks took the *Rule* to Rome. Slowly its tentacles spread throughout Christian Europe and even beyond. It overwhelmed Celtic monastic practice partly because the early Celts followed bizarre tribal rituals that were soon regarded as outdated and inappropriate. The Northumbrian noble Benedict Biscop in the seventh century took the *Rule* of his namesake to the famous monasteries he founded at Wearmouth and Jarrow; later they would house the venerable Bede, author of the *Ecclesiastical History*, who lived under the rule. When Boniface of Wessex organized the Church in the German territories, the Benedictine Rule was familiar enough that it needed no adjective; it was simply "the Rule" or "the Holy Rule." Ultimately the Carolingian renaissance during the rule of Charlemagne (768-814), which involved the systematization and ordering of liturgy and practice throughout the empire, guaranteed the institutionalization of Benedict's Rule.

The rule endured, with slight adaptations that Benedict would not have resisted, right through the Middle Ages down to modern times. In the late Middle Ages the shift from feudalism to urban life reduced the importance of the Rule by diminishing the relevance of monastic life in general. Monasteries were badly hurt as the economic base shifted from rural areas to cities, as secular princes sought to tax and regulate them to death, and as diseases and plagues swept Europe, felling monks in droves. Moreover, corruption and lassitude set in at some of the monasteries, although problems were often dealt with through reform movements spearheaded by the devout.

The new ideology of the eighteenth century, which we may call rationalism, ultimately destroyed the monasteries. It was the premise of rationalism that institutions were only good to the extent that they make themselves useful; thus the Austrian monasteries of Joseph II were obliged to undertake parish and school work to avoid closure. Secular rulers felt free to confiscate Church property in the name of the "public good." In France the revolution of liberty, equality, and fraternity destroyed the most autonomous, egalitarian, and brotherly institution of its time; the monasteries were systematically shut down so that, by the time of Napoleon, there were less than fifty monasteries, down from hundreds that littered Europe since early Christian times.

History can wipe out structures, but ideas live on. Benedict's *Rule* stands as a clear and beautiful testament to a time when countless men and women believed so deeply in Christian truth that they gave up their secular lives in order to pursue that truth in the monastery. Through the regularity and order of the Benedictine Rule, many of those men and women discovered true liberty of mind and spirit. The *Rule* is, ultimately, a great charter of spiritual emancipation.

anselm's

proslogion

ANSELM'S *Proslogion* contains a proof for the existence of God which is perhaps the most original, startling, and — some would say — outrageous that has ever been conceived. Nevertheless Saint Anselm's so-called "ontological argument" has exerted an enormous influence on the subsequent history of philosophy, both Christian and secular. Thomas Aquinas was unimpressed by Anselm's argument, but later medievals found it compelling and provocative. Among lay philosophers Anselm has been engaged by René Descartes, Gottfried Wilhelm Leibniz, and Immanuel Kant. In the twentieth century Anselm has been taken up with renewed interest by thinkers as diverse as Karl Barth and Étienne Gilson.

The appeal of Anselm's proof is that, unlike proofs adduced by Aquinas and others, it does not depend on external objects in nature at all. Anselm does not even assume that natural objects exist in reality, as opposed to merely in the imagination. Critic Arthur McGill observes that "Anselm establishes God's existence not from the visible things of nature or from a knowledge of the divine essence itself, but from an idea of God which we have in our understanding." Somehow, Anselm says, whether we regard ourselves as atheists or agnostics or believers, we have in our heads a certain idea of God that is an important clue to establishing — and understanding — God's necessary existence.

Anselm was born in 1033 in the kingdom of Burgundy, now part of Italy. His mother died when he was quite young, and it devastated him. He became a wandering soul, entering the abbey of Notre Dame at Bec in Normandy in 1059. His curiosity about Bec focused on its prior, a fellow Italian named Lanfranc, who gave the house its reputation for lively intelligence and brilliant controversy. Anselm was himself of alert mind, although with inordinate humility he observes that he chose Bec because he knew that Lanfranc's mental powers would totally overshadow him, leaving him to meditate upon God without distraction. Anselm soon distinguished himself at Bec, however, and when Lanfranc migrated to another part of the country, to found more monasteries, Anselm succeeded him as prior. He held that post for fifteen years, from 1063 until 1078, when he was named abbot of the monastery. During Anselm's tenure Bec's prestige blossomed even more than it did under Lanfranc; its international reputation established it as one of the finest and most demanding intellectual centers in Europe. Anselm routinely corresponded with the great figures of his time — Matilda, countess of Tuscany; the earl of Orkney; Baldwin, king of Jerusalem. When William the Conquerer lay dying at Rouen in 1087 he summoned Anselm to hear his confession.

A prolific writer, Anselm never let his monastery administrative duties interfere with his literary and philosophical output. He published his *Meditations* first, then the *Monologian* and *Proslogion*, followed by another philosophical examination, *De Veritate*. Anselm's most famous theological analysis is the *Cur Deus Homo*, although he also wrote commentaries on Scripture and the sacraments. True to the temper of his time, Anselm penned a number of stinging rebukes to dissenters and heretics, in this case extreme nominalists who tended to deny the real existence of spiritual beings. It is easy to see that, by the end of his life, Anselm had added substantially to the literary store at Bec, which previously had a library of one hundred sixty-four volumes — considered lavishly stocked for that time. Anselm's biographer Eadmer tells us that Anselm's writings and teachings gained their following because he proceeded "not as others do, but in a vastly different way, explaining each point by referring to common and well-known examples, and basing it on solid arguments, without any ornaments or tricks of speech."

Anselm's thought is difficult for modern taxonomy. We are accustomed to think in terms of philosophy versus theology, reason versus revelation, argument versus poetry. Anselm's vision was both substantively and artistically integrated; he refused to let his thoughts navigate fixed categories; he believed that we should worship and argue and exhort, all with the same breath. Consequently Anselm's *Proslogion* is constantly interrupting its reasoning to give vent to a prayer or apostrophe to God. The great tract even begins devotionally:

Come now, little man,
Turn aside for a while from your daily employment,
Escape for a moment from the tumult of your thoughts,
Put aside your weighty cares,
Let your burdensome distractions wait,
Free yourself awhile from God,
And rest awhile in Him.

These decoys are reminiscent of Saint Augustine's *Confessions*, and indeed Anselm acknowledges his tremendous debt to Augustine. From Augustine, in large part, Anselm draws Neoplatonic concepts baptized into an orthodox Christian framework. Yet he cross-fertilizes these with a strong rationalist strain, derived from Aristotle and Boethius and the burgeoning scholastic tradition. It is a mistake to conclude, with critics such as Karl Barth, that Anselm's proof for God's existence was not intended to stand on the basis of its logic — rather, that it was a devotional exercise aimed merely at cheerleading the already converted. That is not how Anselm understood his proof at all. He believed that while faith was necessary to get an understanding of divine things, nevertheless that understanding could then be communicated in wholly human and secular terms. Anselm believed in reason, sharing Augustine's dictum that God could not despise reason, since it is reason that makes man superior to the rest of creation. Indeed Anselm was confident that he could prove not just God's existence but also a number of his attributes — he proceeds to do so in *Proslogion*. Gaunilo of Marmoutier, who rebutted Anselm's proof of God, himself understands it as making a claim on behalf of reason, and Anselm in replying to Gaunilo does not point out that Gaunilo has misread his intention. Therefore, we should understand that *Proslogion* is addressed to believers and nonbelievers alike, all who are capable of reasoned understanding, and show interest in things higher than themselves.

The *Monologion*, which Anselm wrote first, was not a voluntary enterprise; Anselm tells us that he only relented to write it "at the pressing entreaties of brethren." Anselm was often, in life, being drawn reluctantly into things. In 1093, for example, he flatly refused to be named bishop of Canterbury; his biographer Eadmer tells us that the episcopal staff had to be thrust into his hands and he had to be dragged by force to the church to be inducted into office. The *Proslogion*, however, was Anselm's own idea and inspiration. He tells us in his preface that, faced with numerous arguments for God's existence, he sought to discover "one single argument" that would settle the issue. Moreover, it would not rely on sense data but rather "for its proof would need no other save itself." Such a decisive, all-encompassing argument "eluded my acutest thinking completely," Anselm says, "so that finally, in desperation, I was about to give up what I was looking for as something impossible to find." Then it came to him, and "in spite of my unwillingness and my resistance to it, it began to force itself upon me more and more pressingly."

Here Anselm anticipates reader response to his ontological proof. At first, it seems ridiculous and unbelievable, and we resist Anselm's mode of reasoning. But, after a set of deft twists and turns, the argument concludes and we are left a bit breathless, as though victims of some sort of polemical judo. Once we think about what Anselm maintains, and read various commentaries and refutations, we develop a deeper comprehension and respect for Anselm's proof. Now it is not its whiff of originality alone that commends it but also its elusive quality — how irksomely difficult it is to refute and vanquish. We begin to see how great deductive thinkers such as Descartes and Leibniz regarded Anselm's proof as unanswerable and developed their own variations on it. At the very least Anselm forces us to come to terms with deductive reasoning of a very subtle and high order.

Let us get to the argument itself. Anselm begins with

a common definition of God. God is "that than which no greater can be thought." Presumably this is a fairly reasonable and widely accepted definition. We all understand the idea of God to correspond to a supreme being, a being that stretches — even transcends — the limits of our consciousness. Anselm proceeds to say that since we acknowledge and understand this definition, we must have some image of God in our mind. By this he does not mean a pictorial representation; he merely means that our mind comprehends the idea of God as "that than which no greater can be thought."

But if this is true, Anselm says, then God exists. We have proved God's existence. Why? Because if "something than which no greater can be thought" exists in the mind, then it must exist in reality. The reason is that to exist in reality is, according to Anselm, "greater" than to exist merely in the mind. He gives the example of a portrait painter, whose portrait, actually painted, is the realization of a mere fancy or idea in its head; thus the actual painting is "greater" than the mere image of it. In the same way, in order for "that than which no greater can be thought" to satisfy its own definition, it must exist. Otherwise it would be "that than which a greater *can* be thought."

Aware that he has produced something of a stunner, Anselm reinforces his argument with a case that God not only exists, but he cannot be thought not to exist. The reason is that "that which cannot be thought not to exist" is by definition greater than that which may exist, but which can be thought not to exist. Since God is "that than which no greater can be thought," he exists necessarily. If he existed only by fact but not by necessity, he would be a great being indeed, but he would not be "that than which no greater can be thought."

We see, thus, that conceding Anselm's definition leads to an acceptance of God's existence and the inconceivability of his nonexistence. But Anselm is not finished. He proceeds to derive God's attributes from this. Since God is "that than which no greater can be thought," and greater refers to all the virtues, therefore "what good can be lacking to the highest good, through whom all other good exists?" So God is perfectly just, true, blessed, "and whatever it is better to be than not to be."

It is just for God to both punish and pardon the wicked because "when you punish the wicked, this is just — that is what they deserve; but when you pardon them, this is also just, not because of their [just] deserts, but because it comports well with your goodness. For in sparing the wicked you are just according to your own nature, not according to ours." Why should God be good to wicked people? "For you will be less good if you were kind to none of the wicked, because better is he who is good to both evil and good men, than he who is only good to good men. And better is he who is good to the wicked by both punishing them and sparing them, than he who only punishes them." Thus it is understandable and reasonable that "that than which is no greater can be thought" should behave in this manner.

Anselm proceeds in this way, spinning ever-more-intricate syllogisms about the divine nature from his original proposition. Only toward the end does he pause to concede that "reason certainly cannot comprehend why through your supreme goodness you should save some, and through your supreme justice condemn others, which are both equally evil." Finally Anselm has acknowledged a theological item outside the parameters of reason and logic; the reader heaves a sigh of relief, having expected him to be demonstrating allegiance to the Church magisterium very soon as a natural outgrowth of "that than which no greater can be thought."

With a bold flourish, the *Proslogion* ends with a paean to the Almighty. "You are that being who exists truly and simply, because you neither were nor will be but always and already are, nor can you be thought not to be at any time. You are life and light, wisdom and blessedness, eternity and all other good things, indeed you yourself are nothing other than the one and highest good, entirely sufficient to yourself, needing nothing, but he whom all things need for their being and well-being." Not bad as a conclusion for a few pages of tightly reasoned argument.

At this point the reader experiences his first exhilaration over Anselm's argument, quickly followed by qualms and pangs and doubts. The first derives from the Bible itself, from Psalm 14:1, which notes that the fool has said in his heart, "There is no God." How can this be, if God's existence is obvious and a necessary product of our definition of him? Anselm maintains that while the fool may deny God's existence his denial is necessarily irrational — perhaps this is why he is called "the fool." Because, Anselm elaborates, "No one who understands what God is can think that God does not exist, even though he may say these words in his heart." Anselm's point is that saying these words doesn't make them mean anything; they are nothing more than a futile and irrational outburst on the part of the fool.

In his rebuttal to Anselm, Gaunilo makes a point that perhaps strikes closer to our hearts. He says that there are "all kinds of unreal things" that exist in our mind without existing in reality at all. For instance, think of unicorns, yellow flying dogs, mermaids, dragons, giants.

Can we not, in our minds, form images of these beings? Yet will anyone maintain that because we imagine them, therefore they exist? Gaunilo accuses Anselm of an illicit transition from the conceptual to the existential.

Here Gaunilo gives his famous example of the Lost Island. Imagine, he says, an island blessed with "all manner of priceless riches and delights in abundance," superior to all other lands and islands that men inhabit. Now what if someone maintains that this is undoubtedly the most excellent island that we can imagine; since it is excellent beyond all others, and since it exists in our mind, therefore it exists in reality also, in fact it must exist, and let us charter a boat and head for it right away. "I should either think that he was joking," Gaunilo writes, "or I should find it hard to decide which of us I ought to judge the bigger fool — I, if I agreed with him, or he, if he thought that he had proved the existence of this island with any certainty." Here Gaunilo is convinced that he has refuted Anselm.

But Anselm is ready and, in his answer to Gaunilo, replies that Gaunilo has misunderstood him. *Of course* Anselm does not claim that which we imagine in our heads always and necessarily exists in reality. He merely insists that "that than which no greater can be thought," if we can comprehend it, exists and exists by necessity. In other words Anselm's proof is only good in this particular case. It is precisely the character of "that than which no greater can be thought" to exist necessarily; there is nothing in the definition of unicorns and green giants that confers existence on them, much less necessary existence. This also applies to lost islands; with a slight grin, Anselm observes that "I truly promise that if anyone should discover for me something existing either in reality or in mind alone — except that than which no greater can be thought — to which the logic of my argument would apply, then I shall find the Lost Island and give it, never more to be lost, to that person."

Perhaps the most tricky objections to Anselm's argument focus on language, on the meaning of terms and phrases that comprise his syllogism. Gaunilo himself raises a definitional quibble. In what sense do we understand God to be "that than which no greater can be thought"? Gaunilo maintains that while it is true that we understand the words in this definition, it is going too far to say that we comprehend the definition itself. "I do not have any kind of clear and distinct notion of what has been said. Thus, I do not know what is meant or signified by the formula, nor whether there is anything corresponding to it in reality."

Here Anselm is liable to put in a charge of cheating. You agreed to my definition, he might say; now that I've got you, you pretend that it does not make sense. Who says that we have to picture every concept in order to understand it? Life includes a number of definitions and ideas — such as differential equations — that are perfectly comprehensible without any link to either distinct images or real objects. Anselm returns to his point that if we admit the premise that what exists in the mind alone, then God, who is "that than which no greater can be thought," exists by necessity. Either that or we are caught in a self-contradiction from which there is no escape.

Ultimately the best refuge of Anselm's critic is to challenge his claim that reality is somehow "greater" than image. In his *Monologion* Anselm maintains that a horse is "more perfect" than a tree. But what on earth does this mean? It makes sense to compare particular attributes. For example, we may say that, as far as physi-

54

cal strength is concerned, men are in general superior to women. We may also say that, with respect to intuition about personality, women are in general superior to men. But these specific comparisons do not justify an absolute claim that man is superior to woman, or woman is superior to man.

Comparisons of a general or absolute nature become especially baffling when they cut across different species, or involve living versus nonliving things. Human beings are certainly more intelligent than horses, but they certainly cannot run faster than them. A horse is superior to a tree when it comes to mobility, but not when it comes to making fruit, or sheltering birds. By attempting the absolute ranking of creatures in objects implied in such statements as "a horse is more perfect than a tree" Anselm may well be accused of comparing the incomparable — comparing apples and oranges, to use the popular phrase.

A further point is that it doesn't seem to make sense to compare that which exists in the mind to that which exists in the real world. One critic gives the example of a hundred dollars in the mind, as opposed to a hundred dollars in the pocket. Certainly it makes no difference whether I am simply thinking dollars, or whether I am in actual possession of them. But while I may prefer to have the one hundred dollars, does it really make sense for me to say that one hundred dollars in my pocket is, in absolute terms, *greater* than a hundred dollars in my head?

The problem here is one of thinking of existence as a property or attribute. Only if existence is an additional good can it be viewed to contribute to the greatness of "that than which no greater can be thought." The philosopher Immanuel Kant argues that the concept of a possible one hundred dollars and the concept of an actual one hundred dollars are identical. In other words we add nothing to the property of a thing by declaring that it exists. "Existence is not a predicate," is Kant's famous dictum that was, for a long time, considered the final sinking of Anselm's ontological argument.

But again Anselm is not without some counterpunches of his own. First of all, it is not quite true that objects of different qualities are impossible to compare, except in particular respects. Certainly that is not the presumption on which we live life on this earth. We feel free, for instance, to eat venison because we assume that we enjoy dominion over the beasts of the earth. This is not excessively arrogant, since the deer does not shrink from eating other living things, namely various plants, including the bark of trees. Thus even the instinct of the deer seems to confirm nature's hierarchy. The fact that trees grow taller than deer, or the fact that deer run faster than men, neither effectively challenges nature's basis for general assignment of dominion of authority. Further, even if this point doesn't hold, even if comparisons cannot be justified except in particular respects, this does not apply to "that than which no greater can be thought," since when we think of God we think of perfection in *all* attributes.

In reply to Kant, Anselm could say that if something exists, then it is naturally possible for it to exist. Moreover, if something exists necessarily, then by definition it exists. We may infer from this that existence confers on objects both possibility and actuality, which is greater than mere possibility. Similarly, necessary existence confers on objects both necessity and existence, which is greater than mere existence. Why, therefore, is it wrong to maintain that existence, indeed necessary existence, must enhance "that than which no greater can be thought" if it is to remain "that than which no greater can be thought"?

Anselm could add that he is not comparing God existing in reality with God existing in the imagination. If he were, then he could be accused of mistaking existence to be a predicate or quality of an object, which it is not. But in fact Anselm says that God *can be thought* to exist in reality, and this greater than the mere concept of God existing only in the imagination. In other words, a concept involving real existence is superior to a concept that does not. Nothing in Kant suggests that such a comparison between two concepts is invalid.

Again, Kantians have been holding Anselm to a general principle when he is careful to point out that his argument applies only in one special and specific case. Perhaps "existence is not a predicate" for our material universe, but it is Anselm's claim that existence is a necessary element for the concept of God to be meaningful. Remarks philosopher Charles Hartshorne, in his famous commentary on Anselm: "That the idea of God must be an exception to otherwise invalid generalizations is obvious from any usual definition of this idea and has been asserted by many hundreds of philosophers and theologians for nearly 2,000 years. . . . If then we reject the proof simply because it treats the object of worship as an exception to ordinary principles, we shall be declaring not only that the ontological argument for theism is invalid but that theism itself is logically impossible." In other words, we are committed to the position that God is defined as a supernatural being; therefore, he transcends natural laws, and since we only recognize beings and objects that restrict themselves to natural laws, therefore God's existence is impossible. Few thinkers committed to reason would find such atheist dogmatism satisfying.

What Anselm is really saying is that, for all of creation, existence is not a necessity. We exist because we are created, we are generated from the seed or from the womb; we are contingent beings. God, however, exists necessarily. He is not contingent or dependent. How could he be, and still satisfy our definition of God? Thus it is not peculiar or startling to say that we are not going to demand of God that he satisfy human or natural requirements of contingency. Our very conception of God as a perfect being or an eternal being or an omnipotent and omniscient being allows God to stand outside the orbit of typical human or natural experience. "Anselm's real argument," Hartshorne concludes, "is that the merely contingent exemplification of the unique predicate, divinity, would be contradictory, for contingent existence is an inferior mode of existing, suitable only to a creature, not the creator. Hence that-to-which-a-superior-cannot-be-conceived can exist only noncontingently." Leibniz put it even more clearly: "Take away existence from among the elements in the idea of a perfect being, and the idea becomes either the idea of a nonentity or the idea of an idea, and not the idea of a perfect being at all." Leibniz offered his own succinct formulation: "Assuming that God is possible, He exists."

There is no doubt that, in the Neoplatonic environment of Anselm's day, the notion of "greater" and "lesser" comparisons between objects and beings had wider acceptance. Plato advanced his doctrine of Forms or Ideas, which he said were ethereal spirits, somewhere out there in the universe. Material beings were imperfect replications of these perfect forms, linked to them by what Plato called "participation." This Neoplatonic framework, accepted by the early medieval Christians, involved a hierarchical conception of reality; thus it made perfect sense to speak of "degrees of perfection," to locate objects and beings on the cosmic scale, and to identify "that than which no greater can be thought" as the all-encompassing Form or Idea of perfection.

There is an impressive charity of spirit in the debate between Anselm and Gaunilo, despite its feistiness. Gaunilo, after savaging Anselm's proof, nevertheless concludes his analysis by noting that "the other parts of this tract are argued so truly, so brilliantly, so splendidly, with so fragrant a perfume of devout and holy feeling, that in no way should they be rejected because of those claims at the beginning — rightly intuited but less surely argued out. Rather these claims should be demonstrated more firmly so that everything can be received with very great respect and praise." For his part Anselm thanks Gaunilo for doing him the credit and justice of taking his views seriously. "Since you have praised those parts that appeared to you worthy of acceptance," he writes to Gaunilo, "it is quite clear that you have criticized those parts that seemed to you to be weak, not from any malice but from goodwill."

Anselm spent the latter part of his life in fierce and perennial dispute with King William Rufus. The reason for the tension was that Anselm firmly believed, and argued publicly, that the Catholic Church is not a creature of the state; in spiritual terms, the Church is the instrument of God on earth for all people, including the king. During the Investiture controversy Anselm opposed the king's alleged right to invest bishops with their insignia, warning of excommunication as a penalty.

In 1097 Anselm went to Rome without the king's permission and was not permitted to return. He became an exile in his homeland, although in Rome he was a celebrity. Pope Urban II gave him a special seat at the Council of Bari in 1098 and at the Easter Council in Rome the following year. At Bari, Anselm rebutted some Greek theologians who maintained the heresy that the Holy Spirit proceeded from God the Father but not the Son. In 1100 William Rufus was killed and the new king, Henry I, asked Anselm to return to his see. But Anselm was no more pliant toward Henry and in 1103, when he made another unauthorized trip to Rome, Anselm was once again prevented from returning. He spent the rest of his days in Canterbury.

Throughout his life Anselm brought his strong personality and distinctive style to bear on the philosophical and practical issues of the Middle Ages. We find, in his letter to Gunhilda, upbraiding her for adultery with one Count Alan, no hint of euphemism — even though the count is dead. "You loved Count Alan Rufus and he you," Anselm writes. "Where is he now? What has become of the lover you loved? Go and lie now with him in the bed where he lies; gather his worms into your bosom; embrace his corpse; kiss his bare teeth from which the flesh has fallen. He does not now care for your love in which he delighted when he lived; and the flesh which you desired now rests."

Yet Anselm's firmness derives not from a lack of appreciation for love, not from a shortage of passion, but from an excess of it — passion directed at God. He prays in the *Proslogion*:

Let me seek by desiring you,
And desire you by seeking you,
Let me find you by loving you,
And love you in finding you.

Even in his prayers one sees the same rhetorical style that Anselm uses in his arguments. He makes economic use of language, and relishes verbal inversions and antithesis. The purpose of preliminary prayer, Anselm believed, was to cleanse the "spiritual torpor" from the soul that inhibits it from active understanding.

Anselm died at the age of seventy-six in the sixteenth year of his episcopal reign. Eadmer narrates that, as he awaited the end, one of the monks told him, "Father, as far as it is given to us to know, you are leaving this world." Anselm replied, "If it is His will, I shall gladly obey, but if He should prefer me to stay with you just long enough to solve the question of the origin of the soul which I have been turning over in my mind, I would gratefully accept the chance, for I doubt whether anybody else will solve it when I am gone."

john of the cross's
dark night of the soul

WHEN the Bible commands us to "die unto ourselves" for the sake of God, what can it possibly mean? At some superficial level clearly we are being asked to subdue our sinful human nature, and to allow God to replace it with his own divine nature. After all, we were created in his image but have, since the fall, faced the perennial problem of how to recover and repair our relationship with our maker. Saint John of the Cross, the Spanish mystic, wrote a book that, perhaps more than any other, penetrates the infinite distance separating the human from the divine. His *Dark Night of the Soul* "soars on the wings of divine love," according to one critic. It is perhaps the richest, most profound mystical reflection ever written. Since the sixteenth century it has frightened, delighted, and mesmerized readers who have found it speaking to their deepest spiritual longings and quests. John of the Cross has some particularly relevant insights for Catholics and Protestants today.

In John's time Christianity was reacting against some of the dry and ultimately meaningless speculations of the medieval scholastics, who were occupied in considering such questions as whether a cannibal, whose body was wholly composed of material of other human beings, could be said to enjoy a corporal and spiritual existence wholly independent of the people who comprised his meals. Religion is to be "lived, not debated," Erasmus said, and countless people agreed wholeheartedly. But the reaction against scholastic precision ran the risk of degenerating into a radically individualistic faith in which private revelations and communications with God, even when incoherent and contradictory, would be held in higher regard than the enduring principles of faith, handed down by the Apostles and reinforced by the test of tradition and time. A feverish sect called the Illuminists, or Illuminati, claimed to have discovered an interior, more deeply spiritual Christianity, several of its adherents regularly finding themselves suspended in midair or possessed of long-lasting ecstasies. Against this body of experience, some of it profound, much of it contrived and dubious, the Church unleashed the Inquisition, which was charged with separating authentic spiritual truth from chicanery. John's experience should be understood as both continuous with the spiritual striving of his day, as well as thoroughly consistent with orthodoxy. In fact John of the Cross showed that the richest and deepest spiritualism is the fire of orthodoxy; dissident furies are less vivid, more diffuse, less enduring.

He was born in 1542 at Fontiveros, near Ávila in Spain. John's father died when he was quite young, so he came under the aegis of one Don Antonio Alveres de Toledo, who sponsored his studies as well as his training for holy orders. John is described as agile, furtive, and emaciated, barely five feet tall, but striking for his dark and peering eyes. Whatever he undertook he pursued with total dedication and fervor.

After a brief period of study at the Jesuits' College of Medina and the University of Salamanca, John was ordained in 1567. That year he met Teresa of Ávila. He told her that he wanted to live a life of renunciation as a Carthusian. She convinced him to become a Carmelite and join her in a collaborative effort to set up houses across Spain. Immediately John of Saint Mathias, as he was then called, put on the outfit of the Carmelites — a rough tunic, scapular, leather girdle, and white mantle of our Lady — and set to work.

First he helped to found the first male Carmelite house at Durelo in 1568. Others soon followed as people were irresistibly drawn to the austere grandeur of "Fray Juan," or Brother John. He introduced the custom of Perpetual Adoration, which quickly spread throughout Spain. His own asceticism was exemplary; he always went beyond the requirements of the Benedictine Rule and once went so far as to scourge himself bloody for taking a morsel of food before the usual dinnertime. The reason he had taken the food was because he felt faint.

The manifest holiness and dedication of these Carmelites, far from inspiring applause, brought envy and resentment from other religious, including a number of other Carmelites. Much of their anger was directed against Teresa of Ávila, but because she was regarded as protected and untouchable, they settled on John as the scapegoat, accusing him of heresy and association with the Illuminati. The Inquisition was stuck on him, although it never came up with anything incriminating. Between 1575 and 1577 John was twice kidnapped and imprisoned by enemies of Teresa and her Discalced Carmelites. He was bound in a refectory and subjected to the discipline of each friar in the house administering one stroke per day. He was subjected to endless questioning on the pretext of ascertaining his orthodoxy. The first time John was taken captive he was freed through the intercession of the papal nuncio, but the second time he had to engineer a harrowing escape to a nearby Carmelite convent, where the nuns sheltered him. Following his imprisonment John adopted a new name: John of the Cross.

Prison helped him concentrate his mind, however, and he composed a number of the stanzas of his *Spiritual Canticle* with chains around his feet. From 1581 through 1588 John served as prior of Los Maritres, where he worked continuously on the *Dark Night of the Soul* as well as other prose treatises. In 1588 he was named prior of Segovia, as well as the first definitor and *consilario* to the reform in Madrid. He died in 1591. John was beatified by Pope Clement X in 1675, canonized by Pope Benedict XIII in 1726, and declared a Doctor of the Church by Pope Pius XI as late as 1926.

The unsuspecting reader who takes up John's spiritual classic may be surprised, having no expectation of the incandescent energy, the molten passion, that floods the *Dark Night of the Soul*. Saint John begins with a warning. The "dark night" he speaks of refers to the cleansing, or purgation, of the two dimensions of man's nature — his senses and his spirit. The night of the senses is "bitter and terrible to taste," he says, "wherein the sense is subdued to the spirit," but it is an anguish reserved for beginners. The night of the soul, by contrast "bears no comparison to it, for it is horrible and awful to the spirit," and its agonies are complicated by the fact that it is unfamiliar and unknown — "Very little has been said of this," John writes, "and very little is known of it, even by experience." The reader has the acute sense of being led down a dank and chilling path, where goose bumps may be expected and whose contours are not going to be entirely pleasant.

Why would a loving God subject his creation to a "dark night" of suffering? Why, indeed, would he single out those who seek his wisdom and his ways for what John clearly regards as physical and mental torment and anguish? The ancient philosophers had an explanation: God is playfully malevolent, and derives cruel amusement from the misbegotten travails of his creation. Shakespeare reflected this pagan view when he wrote, "As flies to wanton boys are we to the gods. They kill us for their sport."

The Christian explanation, echoed by John of the Cross, is different. God's infinite benevolence must somehow be reconciled with his infinite justice. Thus God must find a way to love man, while at the same time judging him. Here is God's problem: man's sin has created an impassable chasm between the human and the divine, for how can God, who is pure, have anything to do with evil? The Christian answer is that God, through the redemptive act of his Son, Jesus, undertakes to purify the corrupt human soul, to restore it to its erstwhile health, and to unite it with himself. While this is primarily God's undertaking — John stresses the "passive nature" of the human soul in these transactions — nevertheless it involves a great heaving and searing and cleansing for us mortals. It is not surprising if we feel a bit like a pile of dirty clothes being hurled and tossed about in the hot, steamy water and claustrophobic environment of a washing machine.

Initially, says John, "The soul, after it has been converted to the service of God, is spiritually nurtured and caressed by God, just as the tender child is warmed and carried by its loving mother in the nest of her bosom, tended with sweet milk and fondling." But, he adds, "As the child grows bigger, the mother gradually ceases caressing and, hiding her tender love, puts bitter aloes upon her sweet breast, sets down the child from her arms, and makes it walk upon its feet, so that it may lose the habits of a child and occupy itself with more important and substantial occupations." So, too, the Christian initiate must develop and grow in his new life with God, in order to fully understand what it means to be one with the supernatural.

Those who first accept Christ may feel that their lives have been transformed, and their obstacles to grace and salvation removed, but John tempers their enthusiasm by pointing out a catalog of follies and faults that continue to plague what he calls "beginners." Somewhat with alarm, the beginner discovers that his residual evils are not trivial at all; indeed they correspond to the seven deadly sins. For example:

• *Pride*: Beginners tend to consider themselves superior because they have found the light. "They speak of spiritual things in the presence of others, and seek to teach such things rather than to learn them." They can become hostile to Church authority. "When their spiritual superiors do not approve of their vanity, they consider that they do not understand them, or because they do not approve of this or comply with that, their confessors and superiors are themselves not spiritual." Beginners often are flamboyant in their performance of good deeds. "In these persons the devil often increases their fervor so they perform these works more frequently, but thus their pride and presumption only grows greater. For the devil knows quite well that these works and virtues are not only useless to them, but even become vices in them . . . when they are not done for the greater joy of God." John of the Cross likens these men to Pharisees, swollen with vanity and religiosity, but eventually without that true religious kinship with God that breeds humility and is only sustained in humility.

• *Wrath*: Beginners often become very judgmental and impatient with others, regarding them as backward and insufficiently enlightened from the truth. "They condemn others in their heart, when they see that they have not the kind of devotion which they themselves desire," John points out. Further, "They become irritated at the sins of others, and keep watch on them with a sort of uneasy zeal." Sometimes this wrath is even turned inward: "Beginners become anguished when they see themselves falling into sin, thinking themselves to be saints already; thus they become angry and intolerant toward themselves." Thus is the sin of wrath intermingled with the sin of pride.

• *Luxury*: Beginners are often attracted to the lavish and exhibitionistic features of Christianity. "They are at times apt to fall into certain ecstasies, in public rather than in secret, wherein the devil aids them, and they are pleased that this should be noticed, and are often eager that it should be noticed more." John does not object to spiritual experience, by any means, but when it is reduced largely to sensual experience — yelling and screaming and dancing in the aisles — he worries about its "inebriating effect." Finally, emotional histrionics are part of the devil's tactic "to disquiet and disturb the soul when it is at prayer or striving to pray."

• *Gluttony*: Saint John warns that beginners can so relish the initial pleasure and sweetness of spiritual exercises that "they strive more after spiritual sweetness than after spiritual purity and discretion." In other words, they value experience over truth. They seek not so much God as divine feelings and sentiments. Sometimes this has perversely sensual effects — "and some of these persons, attracted by the pleasure they find therein, kill themselves with fasts, and perform more than their frailty can bear, and more than they have been commanded." Here John is gently faulting the monks of an earlier day who plunged into ecstasies of self-flagellation and self-mortification, or the Christians of our own day who luxuriate in gluttonous experience of a different sort: "They think that all the business of prayer consists in experiencing sensible pleasure and devotion and they strive to obtain this by great effort, wearying and fatiguing their faculties and their heads, and when they have not found pleasure they become greatly discouraged, thinking that they have accomplished nothing." John is making a plea for spiritual discipline, temperance, and sobriety.

The point about these and other sins that beginners fall into is that human beings do not cease to be human beings when they decide to accept Christ. All they have willed is that they submit to the majesty and sovereignty of God. But this submission means that they are leaving it up to their Creator to perform, in them, the purgative task that consists of the eradication and stripping of all evil taints and tinctures from their senses and spirits. "God now sees that the beginners have grown a little, and they are becoming strong enough to lay aside their swaddling clothes to be taken from the gentle breast, so he sets them down from his arms and teaches them to walk on their own feet, which they feel to be very strange, for everything seems to be going wrong with them."

That, we soon discover, is an understatement. The dark night, when it comes, throws human beings into utter despondency and confusion. "When they are going about these spiritual exercises with the greatest delight and pleasure, and when they believe that the sun of divine favor is shining most brightly upon them, God turns all their light into darkness," according to the *Dark Night of the Soul*. At that point, the believer feels totally alienated not only from God but also from himself and from the world. He feels radically isolated, alone, abandoned.

But how do we know that this feeling does not represent spiritual backsliding, a falling away from the early excitement of Christian conversion? John of the Cross offers three criteria to ensure that the beginner is undergoing spiritual surgery and not lapsing into the maladies of his old sinful self.

First, the soul loses all sense of pleasure, either in the material world or in God. After all, part of the divine purpose here is to extinguish in the soul its sensual and corporal desires.

Second, the soul remains centered on God, only it thinks that it is not serving God because it cannot experience his sweetness. This is not to be confused with spiritual lukewarmness, John warns, "for it is the nature of lukewarmness not to care greatly to have any inward solicitude for the things of God." Here God aims to keep the soul riveted on him while denying it the sensual or pleasurable dimensions of that relationship.

"God transfers to the spirit the good things and the strength of the senses," John says. "The sensual part of man has no capacity for that which is pure spirit, and thus, when it is the spirit that receives God's pleasure, the flesh is left without savor. . . . Meanwhile, the spirit, which is being fed, goes forward in strength. If it is not immediately conscious of spiritual sweetness and delight, the reason is the strangeness of the exchange or transfer. Its palate has been accustomed to those other sensual pleasures upon which its eyes are still fixed. The spiritual palate is not ready yet for such subtle pleasure. The purpose of the arid and dark night is to prepare for this."

The third and final sign is that the soul feels a total lack of communication with God. "For God now begins to communicate Himself to it, no longer through sense, as He did before, but by means of pure spirit." From now on, the author of the *Dark Night of the Soul* tells us, imagination and feelings and fancy have no part of the human interactions with God. The conversation is from one spirit to another, a truly transcendent conversation, between two beings, the created and the Creator, the one made in the image of the other.

The Christian believer in this predicament must no doubt feel much like Satan and the wicked angels "hurled headlong flaming from the ethereal sky, with hideous ruin and combustion, down to bottomless perdition," as Milton recounts in *Paradise Lost*. But, says John, cheer up. "It is well for those who find themselves in this condition to take comfort, to persevere in patience, and to be in no way afflicted." They should not have qualms about their passive inaction. They should abide their frustration at not being able to do anything about their confusion and pain. After all, John says, delicate divine operations are being conducted on the soul. "It is just as if some painter were painting or dyeing a face; if the sitter were to move because he desired to do something, he would prevent the painter from accomplishing anything and would disturb him in what he was doing." Thus John counsels the believer to take a spiritual time-out. Don't distract God.

Next, John of the Cross outlines the benefits that ac-

71

crue to the believer who allows himself to be transformed through God's laser of truth and love. The believer is miserable, to be sure, but at least he comes to a full understanding of his own misery. Knowledge of the magnitude of human sin is a necessary prelude to fully embracing God's grace and letting it change our lives. The soul also learns humility before God, John tells us, just as Moses, standing before the burning bush, took off his shoes and fell to the ground. Further, the soul comes to a new appreciation of God's indescribable beauty and grandeur. "Let me know myself, Lord, that I should know Thee," Saint Augustine prayed. Man acknowledges his own sins and failures in the same measure that he acknowledges his dependency on God, and God's transcendent ability to remedy his problems and restore man's wholeness. Finally, John says, "inasmuch as the soul is now purged from the affectations and desires of the sense, it obtains liberty of spirit" and thus "wondrously emancipated from the hands of its three enemies — the devil, the world and the flesh." None of them now has the power to make war on the spirit because the spirit has been delivered from their domain, which is the domain of senses.

At this point John's reader feels a sense of exhilaration but also exhaustion. He has traveled what his guide calls "the long spiritual road." Yet John is only getting started. He has dealt with the purgation of sense, he points out, but what about the purgation of spirit, the second "dark night" that is reputedly more daunting than the first? The ills of the spirit, he says, "are the imperfect habits and affections which have remained all the time in the spirit, and are like roots, to which purgation of sense has been unable to penetrate. The difference between the purgation of these and that of this other kind is the difference between the root of the branch, or between the removing of a stain which is fresh and one which is old and long-standing . . . the purgation of sense is only the entrance and beginning to the purgation of the spirit."

Yet it should be understood that the cleansing of sense and spirit occur simultaneously. John's division is not chronological but conceptual.

There is also a difference of intensity. A repeal of the senses is mentally and emotionally trying, but what is it compared to the "divine [light] assailing the soul . . . the soul feels itself to be perishing and melting away, in the presence and sight of its miseries, in a cruel spiritual death, even as if it had been swallowed by a beast and felt itself being devoured in its belly"? In order to make itself worthy of spiritual resurrection, of union with God who is pure, the soul must endure its "sepulchre of dark death." Here one begins to understand the phrase "dark night," as John of the Cross leads the reader out of twilight and into utter blackness.

Why should a spirit face such difficulty in communicating with God who himself is spirit, John asks, raising the question to answer it. Because the soul has become contaminated through the sin of the fall of man's continued rebellion against God. Thus the soul, when it succumbs to the fiery rays of love, is blinded with pain. "The clearer . . . the light, the more it blinds and darkens the pupil of the owl," the author of the *Dark Night of the Soul* says. "So also the more directly we look at the sun, the greater is the darkness which it causes." Saint Dionysius somewhat curiously referred to God's soul-cleansing as his "ray of darkness," because impure souls have no way of looking God in the eye. A further reason for the soul's pain in its encounter with God is that "when the pure light assails the soul, in order to expel its impurity, the soul feels itself to be so unclean and miserable that it believes God to be against it, and thinks that it has set itself up against God." Job felt this way when he cried out that God had abandoned him: "Why hast Thou set me contrary to Thee?"

Here John is writing at the summit of his rhetorical abilities. His prose is sharp, fiery, vivid. The reader is almost lifted out of his mundane world, and inhaled into an entirely new milieu — one richer, grander, wilder, scarier. Readers who never knew they had a spirit must now, if only empathetically, experience what John calls the "annihilation . . . scorching . . . emptying . . . consuming" of the spirit in a furnace of divine combustion. The author himself warns that this feels "as if a man were suspended or held in the air so that he could not breathe."

These hot fumes, however, do not last forever. In fact, their purpose is to avert the eternal fire that awaits souls who wish to postpone their dark night. "Although our night brings darkness to the spirit, it does so only to give it light in everything," the *Dark Night of the Soul* points out. "Although it humbles the soul and makes it miserable, it does so only to exalt it and to raise it up. Although it impoverishes it and empties it of all natural affection and attachment, it does so only that it may enable it to stretch forward, divinely, and thus to have fruition and experience of all things, both above and below, yet to reserve its unrestricted liberty of spirit."

In an unforgettable image, John of the Cross tells us that "this purgative and loving knowledge or divine light whereof we speak acts upon the soul . . . in the same way as fire acts upon a log of wood in order to transform it into itself. First a fire begins to dry wood, driving out its moisture and causing it to shed the water within itself. Then it begins to make it black, dark and unsightly, and even give forth a bad odor. But as it dries it little by little, it drives away all the dark and unsightly accidents which are contrary to the nature of the fire. Finally, it begins to kindle it externally and give it heat, and at last transforms it into itself and makes it beautiful as fire." So also the divine fire of contemplative love cleanses what John calls the "vicious and evil humors" of sense and spirit, uniting the soul unto itself.

John tells us that he has just given us a vision of what purgatory might be like. There, too, souls must lose their stains and imperfections through fire. "But the fire would have no power over us, even if we came into contact with it, if we have no imperfections for which to suffer. These are the material upon which the fire of purgatory seizes; when that material is consumed there is naught else to burn. So also here, when the imperfections are consumed, the affliction of the soul ceases and fruition remains."

Throughout its agony the soul is continually sustained by God's propellant of love, John tells us. "The property of love is to desire to be united, joined and made equal and like to the object of its love." God's love enkindles in the soul an enduring desire to be fulfilled in union with God. "Thus all the faculties and desires of the soul come to be prepared in such a way as to be able to receive, feel and taste that which is divine and supernatural, after a sublime and lofty manner, which is impossible if the old self die not first of all." This, then, is what Scripture means when it asks us to die unto ourselves. It means that we should submit ourselves to the "dark night" of purgation, in the confident hope of walking in the valley of the sun.

In the last section the author of the *Dark Night of the Soul* discusses the "secret wisdom" of the path he has outlined. Now Christianity is universal and the Gospel urges us to "proclaim the good news," so why the need for secrets? Here as always John is ready with explanations. This knowledge is secret in the sense that it refers to mystical experience, alien to the senses. Thus those who are unwilling to walk outside the orbit of material experience are never going to know the dizzying heights of mystical truth. Further, since mystical knowledge is nonsensory it is, by nature, incommunicable. John in trying to relay it to readers is doing what he himself proclaims to be impossible; to his credit, he succeeds as far as is humanly possible. Finally, the soul itself does not fully comprehend what it receives from God, because "this mystical knowledge has the property of hiding the soul within itself . . . for the language of God has this characteristic that, since it is so intimate and spiritual in its relations with the soul, it transcends every facility and makes all capacity of the outward and inward senses cease to be dumb."

The *Dark Night of the Soul* closes with a blissful account of the soul's ascension up the mystical ladder, reminiscent of upward spirals of Dante's *Paradiso*. Up the rungs of grace we climb, until that rhapsodic summit, "the tenth and last step of this secret ladder of love, where the soul is wholly assimilated to God." Here the soul sees what John calls the "livery of three colors — white, green and purple," denoting the theological virtues of faith, hope, and charity. These forever equip the soul against the temptations of sin, and enable the soul to enter into never-ending communion with the God from whence it came.

F·I·V·E

teresa of ávila's

autobiography

TERESA of Ávila, a contemporary of Saint John of the Cross, was in life very different from the author of the *Dark Night of the Soul*. While John was gaunt, impersonal, and flaming in his prose, Teresa was round, informal, and intensely personal. Not for her the abstract, rarified air of speculation. She wrote in a tone distinctively autobiographical, intimate, and even colloquial. The reader who expects to discover an ascetic is more likely to encounter a face he can virtually recognize. Of Saint Teresa we say what we might of Samuel Johnson after reading Boswell's unforgettable biography; we would recognize them if they walked into a room tomorrow, by their demeanor and personality. Generations of readers have met and gotten to know Teresa of Ávila. As critic Allison Peers remarks, "To Teresa it was given to speak to the world, in her diaphanous language and unaffected style, of the work of the Holy Spirit in the enamored soul, of the interior strife and continual purgation through which a soul must pass in its ascent of Mount Carmel and of the wonders which await it on the mountain's summit."

The familiarity and simplicity of Teresa's *Autobiography* camouflage its richness and depth. It is a book resplendent with divine wisdom, yet not of an abstruse sort. With Teresa, wisdom is joined with affection — the *Autobiography* is throughout irrigated with God's love. While the Christian beginner finds in it spiritual resources to last a long time, the veteran is continually amazed by the maturity of its discernment. Teresa, after all, is always advertising her own foolishness or naïveté. Whenever she describes with unmatched penetration and clarity a spiritual experience, she adds that she is "probably speaking nonsense" and it will be up to her superiors to "correct this account or throw it away." Indeed Teresa says at the outset that she would rather not be writing her autobiography, because "it hinders me from spinning my wheel and . . . I have numerous other things to do." If readers remember her account, she urges them to forget the source in order to give her book credibility. "No one would give credence to this if it were related to one so base and wicked as I."

There are moments when the reader of Teresa's *Autobiography* grows a bit weary of this self-deprecation, suspecting it to be a form of vanity. But these suspicions are continually frustrated and defeated by Teresa's total and uncompromising sincerity. The woman, we realize, really does think she is worthless vermin destined to burn forever in hell. She truly is astonished that God permits her to be a vessel of his love and truth. Teresa is even sexist without embarrassment: "The very thought that I am a woman is enough to make my wings droop — how much more, then, the thought that I am such a wicked one." Approaching the *Autobiography* even from a skeptical or hostile point of view, the reader is forced to conclude that either he is witnessing neurotic hallucination or spiritual experience of a very high order. The first possibility is canceled out by Teresa's acute self-consciousness, even in phases of rapturous abandon; also her sharp sense of irony. "I was ashamed to go to my confessor," she remarks after one of her visions, "for fear that he might laugh at me and say: what a Saint Paul she is, with her heavenly visions! Quite a Saint Jerome." Her wry humanity bursts through when a fellow sister catches her enjoying a fine partridge dinner and reminds her of her vow of simplicity. "There is a time for penance and a time for partridge," Teresa remarks, coolly proceeding with her meal.

The *Autobiography* set the stage — and the principles — for other contemplative classics by Teresa, such as *The Book of Her Life, The Way of Perfection*, and *The Interior Castle*. In addition Teresa wrote mediations on the Songs of Solomon, exclamations for nuns, spiritual maxims, and rulebooks for visitation of her convents. Together all these form a spiritual treasury for joyous reading as well as practical assistance in the way of the cross. As for the *Autobiography*, the jewel in the crown, perhaps not since Saint Augustine's *Confessions* has a book had such a wide and deep impact in turning hearts and souls to God.

Teresa was born in Ávila in Spain on March 28, 1515. Her parents were affluent and well descended; the duke of Navas is quoted as saying that Teresa's lineage is more ancient and distinguished than his own. The history of Ávila is one of war and besiegement; some of this military mentality is reflected in Teresa's writing, as when she says, "Let the contemplative consider what he is doing, for if he lets the standard fall the battle will be lost." During Teresa's life Spanish troops were battling in France, Italy, and the Netherlands; five of her own brothers took part in the battle of Inaquito in 1546.

One of Teresa's keenest early impulses was to

achieve martyrdom in battle with the Moors, a constant threat and plague to Catholics. This aspiration Teresa understood as deriving not from courage but from lack of it: "When I read of the martyrdoms suffered by the saints, I used to think they purchased the fruition of God very cheaply, and I had a desire to die as they had done, not out of any love for God of which I was conscious, but in order to attain as quickly as possible to the fruition of the great blessings which, as I read, were laid up in heaven." Teresa and her brother Rodrigo even planned to run away from home to minister among the Moors, in order that they might be caught and beheaded; fortunately an uncle rescued them from that childish escapade.

Teresa cultivated a fervent attachment to chivalric tales; she even began to write one, although the manuscript is sadly lost. Influenced by the esthetics of Arthurian legend, Teresa writes, "I began to deck myself out and try to attract others by my appearance, taking great trouble with my hands and hair, using perfumes and all other vanities I could get. . . . I was very fastidious." During this period Teresa also accuses herself of learning "every kind of evil" from a family relative. She may have had a romantic relationship during this time; her account is too bashful for us to discover the details. Teresa does tell us that "I thought more about pleasures of sense than of my soul's profit. Even if I read the entire narrative of the Passion, I could not shed a tear."

Then Teresa fell ill. During her recuperation she visited one of her father's brothers, a friar at the Augustinian convent of Our Lady of Grace. He made her read spiritual books to him. Although she was at first lackluster and bored by it all, soon "I began to comprehend the truth, which I had learned as a child, that all things are nothing, and that the world is vanity and will soon pass away." Teresa was being called back to that childlike love of God that Jesus mentions in the Gospels. For the first time she seriously began to consider becoming a nun.

The life of the Spanish clergy and religious was reputed to be a difficult one indeed. While the rest of the Continent was growing progressively more rationalistic and humanistic, everywhere in Spain tales circulated about priests and nuns who locked themselves up in chambers, put on purple robes, and carried heavy crosses as they scourged themselves until tears ran down their cheeks and blood down their backs. Teresa's writing indicates that she found all this at once impressive, intimidating, and very strange. She didn't accept every spectacular self-abnegation as worthy of accolades. "From foolish devotions may God deliver us," she observes. She also reports meeting many who were "saints in their own opinion, but when I got to know them, they frightened me more than all the sinners I have ever met." Teresa's healthy girlishness, her ever-insistent humanity, is crucial to understanding the spiritual attitude of her later experience.

In November, 1536, at the age of twenty-one, Teresa took the habit at the Convent of the Incarnation at Ávila. Most of the time she cleaned kitchens and swept floors, but "there came to me a new joy, which amazed me for I could not understand whence it arose." Teresa's one complaint about the convent was its confessors for the nuns. "What in reality was venial sin, they would tell me it was no sin at all; and the most grievous of mortal sins was to them only venial." This Teresa finds no service to her soul but rather a dangerous deception. "This did me much harm. I speak of it here to warn others against such an evil." Fortunately, she says, a Dominican Father corrected these false foundations and helped her to come to a true appreciation of her faults, and a true repentance.

Throughout her life Teresa was sickly. Her illnesses typically evoked a rush of doctors and Masses as both science and religion worked together to attempt to heal her fragile body. For almost twenty years, from late adolescence to middle age, she is said to have suffered vomiting almost daily — sometimes vomiting had to be induced by tickling her throat with a feather, in order to relieve nausea which racked her whole body. Despite these afflictions Teresa bore herself with remarkable cheeriness and gaiety. She could never stand "gloomy saints," she writes.

In the convent Teresa finds herself falling into "many and grave occasions of sin." No doubt these were venial, in the nature of tiring with the work routine or feeling resentment at the orders of a superior. Nevertheless Teresa is severe with herself. "In my wickedness I was one of the worst people alive," she observes. She is worried about her readers. "I know well that nobody will derive any pleasure from reading about anyone so wicked, and I sincerely hope that those who read this will hold me in abhorrence, when they see that a soul which had received such great favors could be so obstinate and ungrateful."

The mild freedom permitted by occasional relaxation of the rules of the enclosure, Teresa finds wildly permissive and libertine. The nuns gave her too much liberty and not enough stern supervision, she says. "I think it was a very bad thing for me not to be in a convent that was enclosed. The freedom which the sisters, who were good, might enjoy . . . would certainly have led me, who am wicked, down to hell, had not the Lord, through very special favors, using means and remedies which are all His own, delivered me from this peril." Freedom for Teresa is only good insofar as it leads to the truth, who is God.

Teresa's obsession with her own worthlessness should not be understood as total self-abasement. Rather, it is the full recognition of the spiritual helplessness of the human being to address the sin of humankind's fall, repeated and amplified as it is in our own lives. "To be humble is to walk in truth," Teresa writes in the *Interior Castle*. It is this truth that leads to acceptance of the redemptive love of God, without which all the pleasures of the world are, for Teresa, no more than "a few twigs of withered rosemary."

In the second part of her *Autobiography* Teresa offers an analysis of the four kinds of prayer. The profundity of this segment has made it essential reading in the literature of mysticism. Teresa begins with the homespun analogy — that of a garden. A garden can be watered in different ways. The beginner draws the water from the well with a bucket, which is very laborious. A second way is to use a waterwheel, which is less painful and gets more water. A better approach is to use a stream or brook, which saturates the field more thoroughly. But the fourth and best way is through heavy rain, "when the Lord waters the garden with no labor of ours." Prayer with God corresponds to these four ways.

For the beginner, prayer is a burden and an exertion. "Beginners are not always sure that they are repented of their sins," and this is distressing. "Then they have to endeavor to meditate upon the life of Christ and this fatigues their minds." But beginners should take heart, Teresa says, because they would not have the difficulties they experience unless they were sincere and serious in their effort to reach God.

What they should begin to do is relax, and let God adjust the pulleys of their heart and soul. "There are some people who think that their devotion will slip away from them if they relax a little. . . . It is permissible for us to take some recreation in order that we may be stronger when we return to prayer. In everything we need discretion." Teresa even asks that the beginner give his intellect a break; instead of "composing speeches" to God, why not let him know how right he is not to allow you into his full presence?

When we do this, Teresa says, "the understanding loses its power of working, because God suspends it. . . . He gives it something which both amazes it and keeps it busy, so that, without reasoning in any way, it can understand more in a short space of time than we, with all our human efforts, can fathom in many years." Yet we should not voluntarily relinquish our will or reason. "It is essential that we should not try to lift up our spirit unless it is lifted up by the Lord." The maturation of prayer consists in that gradual release which turns over the reins of control from the human being to God.

In the second stage of prayer, Teresa takes back some of her earlier counsel. The believer is stronger now, and must not allow complacency to set in. He or she must thrust forward with full determination. "The devil persuades us that it is pride which makes us have ambitious desires and want to imitate the saints and wish to be martyrs. . . . He induces us to believe that we who are sinners may admire the deeds of the saints but must not copy them." In her own case, Teresa tells us, the devil constantly tempted her by telling her that if she prayed or meditated too hard it would ruin her health, and what good would she be for God then? To this Teresa responded: "Rest indeed! I need no rest, what I need is crosses." As Teresa herself put it elsewhere, there is a time for relaxation and a time for feistiness.

Teresa tells us that our labor of prayer is made easier by God's own intervention, like that of a waterwheel that carries the weight of the bucket. "So little labor is involved that, even if prayer continues for a long time, it never becomes wearisome." God suspends all faculties save the will, "occupied in such a way that, without knowing how, it becomes captive. It allows itself to be imprisoned by God. It has no freedom to love anything but Him." Also, it loses covetousness for things of this world. "It sees clearly that on earth it cannot have a moment of God's joy; there are no riches, no dominions, or honors, or delights which suffice to give us such satisfaction even for the twinkling of an eye. For this is true joy, and the soul realizes that it is this which gives genuine satisfaction."

This delirium, which will not last, is "a little spark of true love for the Lord which He begins to enkindle in the soul so that it should come to understand the nature of His love with its attendant joy." As for us, we are so eager for delectable experience that we cannot get enough. We strive to inhale and consume more. But just then the beautiful taste, the exotic fragrance, begins to disappear, for it was not present by our striving, and our intervention can only interrupt its flow. Nevertheless, once we have experienced God in this direct and personal way, we cannot forget or undo it. God has given us a "sign" or "pledge," Teresa says, that "He is choosing us for great things if we will prepare ourselves to receive them."

A burning desire to make progress in prayer, combined with what Teresa calls "a mature fear which springs from faith," draws us into a third stage of prayer. Here the faculties are totally extinguished or put into a deep sleep. "They retain only the power of occupying themselves wholly with God." We experience "ineffable joy," a "heavenly madness," Teresa says, then continues: "The soul would like to shout praises aloud — it cannot contain itself." She herself "used often to commit follies because of this condition, and to be inebriated with it." Yet, although we do not understand it, what we are acquiring is divine wisdom. For God, wisdom and pleasure are one.

Teresa says she experienced this kind of prayer as "quite definitely a union of the entire soul with God." Distinctions between the active and contemplative approach melt away — the soul is engaged totally, even passively. "Those in this state know that they are not wholly masters of themselves and that the better part of their soul is elsewhere. It is as if we were speaking to one person while somebody else was speaking to us: we cannot be wholly absorbed in either the one conversation or the other."

Both the memory and the imagination are free but disengaged, Teresa says; if this were not the case "one would never believe what turmoil they make and how they try to upset everything." Sin acts this way, too. "It blinds and diverts us in such a way that we cannot do as we would — namely, be always occupied with God."

The fourth and highest degree of prayer is the divine thunderstorm, the rain that waters the field effortlessly, thoroughly. "In this state of prayer there is no feeling, but only rejoicing, unaccompanied by any understanding of the thing in which the soul rejoices. All the senses are occupied in such a way that none of them is free." In fact the soul's exultation can only be experienced, not communicated. "There is no power left in the body or soul to transmit its rejoicing . . . if it can communicate it, then it is not true union, because union is two different things becoming one." If there is any emotion that Teresa experienced during this ecstasy, it is a pang of unworthiness: "O my Creator, pour not such precious liquor into so broken a vessel, for again and again Thou hast seen how I have allowed it to run away."

At these Himalayan heights of spirituality, Teresa began to experience supernatural things. Modern skeptics of a psychological bent have questioned these, attributing them to psychosomatic disorder. If Teresa is suspected of spiritual indulgence, though, her *Autobiography* refutes such a charge. Far from inviting supernatural experience she was dragged, kicking and screaming, into the orbit of the Almighty.

On one occasion, she writes, she was on her knees praying when her whole body began to shake to the point of being lifted off the ground. Several nuns saw her in this state, but she ordered them never to speak of it. "I besought the Lord earnestly not to grant me any more favors which had visible and exterior signs, for I was exhausted by having to endure such worries of detection." Despite Teresa's pleas, however, her spiritual experiences continued, and finally she became resigned to them. "It is a terrible struggle, and to continue it against the Lord's will avails very little, for no power can do anything against His."

Teresa compares this state to that of a little dove, blinded by the light of a divine streak of lightning. The result is astonishment, absorption, and finally true humility, which "never allows one to say anything good of itself, nor will permit others to do so." Ultimately God's light cures even this blindness, however; the ecstasy of slumber leads to a new awakening in the presence of God. "The sun of justice strikes the soul and forces it to open its eyes."

How is one to know that one is truly having an experience of God and not some faked or ersatz experience? Teresa emphasizes the total subservience of the soul to God in cases of genuine communion. "When, on the natural plane, we do not wish to hear, we can close our ears, or attend to something else," she writes, "but when God talks to the soul, there is no such remedy: I have to listen, whether I like it or not." Authentic communication from God, therefore, feels more like listening than like speaking; the soul is the receiver of information, not the composer of it. Moreover, "false locutions affect nothing, whereas when the Lord speaks, the words are accompanied by effects . . . they prepare the soul and make it ready and move it to affection, give it light and make it happy and tranquil." With this as with so many things, we can safely apply the biblical principle: by their fruits you shall know them. When the devil speaks to us, Teresa says, the soul responds with "aridity and disquiet" because the message of Satan is not praise and rejoicing, but rebellion and alienation.

Teresa emphasizes, though, that no matter how sublime or spontaneous one's spiritual experience, in order for it to be authentic it must be congruent with both Scripture and the teaching of the magisterium. "The soul strives ever to act in conformity with the doctrine of the Church," Teresa writes. Also, "The soul is convinced that a thing comes from God only if it is in conformity with Holy Scripture."

A powerful influence on Teresa's life was the mystic Saint Peter of Alcántara. Teresa remembers him with fond admiration in her *Autobiography*. Alcántara lived in a tiny cell, four and a half feet long, which meant that he could not even sleep lying down. He spent his nights sitting, with his head resting on a piece of wood. During winter he left his windows open and braved the bitter elements as a gesture of mortification and sacrifice. Usually he only ate once in three days. He made a practice of never looking at women. "He was so extremely weak that he seems to be made of nothing but roots of trees." After his death, though, Teresa had visions of him. His body was made whole and healthy by the "blessedness of his penance" and Teresa "beheld him in the greatest bliss."

In her spiritual maturity Teresa's visions and divine experiences became more frequent. Once at Mass on the feast of Saint Paul, she saw Christ in his resurrected body. Another time he was wearing a crown of thorns and carrying his cross. Teresa reports that if she tried to see more than what was granted to her, the vision was immediately lost. One spectacular vision involved an angel. He was "not tall — on the contrary, short, but of great beauty, and his face afire." He pierced her heart with a spear of gold with flaming iron at its tip. This caused Teresa pain and she cried out, yet it was such sweet agony that she says she never wants to forget it. This vision, Teresa's most famous, was later ratified by Pope Benedict IX, who instituted the feast of the Transverberation of the Heart of Saint Teresa, a feast observed to this day.

Teresa emphasizes, however, that her wound from the angel was spiritual, not physical. She does not confuse the supernatural with natural experience. Thus one would expect her to be indifferent to scientific skepticism about the transformation of her anatomy — God's interest is in the soul, not the ephemeral flesh. Teresa always resisted the miraculous. She identified with the Catholic saint who said, "I do not want this favor granted to me because I believe firmly enough without the help of wonders." A number of great Catholic spiritual figures have never seen visions; equally, visionaries are not always saints. If they were, Saint Boniface wryly remarks, Balaam and his donkey should be canonized.

Moreover, Teresa's mystical experiences do not rival those of Peter of Alcántara. Perhaps Teresa's most remarkable feat, according to her biographer Bishop Yepes, who knew her well, was to be seized by rapture and lifted into the air, still holding on to some mats that she grabbed to keep her on the ground. Contrast this with Alcántara who, according to a witness at his canonization proceeding, frequently flew to the tops of trees uttering weird shrieks and terrifying his brethren.

Teresa was aware of the excesses of peasant superstition, discovering miracles in merely natural phenomena. On Christmas Eve in 1577 she broke her arm on the way to the choir; when the nuns unanimously proclaimed this the devil's work Teresa retorted, "Nonsense, the devil would do much worse than that." She believed that supernatural experience always served a purpose of education or growth. Once at Mass she saw two devils gripping the throat of a celebrant, but the host was uncontaminated; Teresa better understood that the sinfulness or corruption of a priest does not invalidate the sacrament.

Teresa's concern, even more than with the devil seen in visions, was the unseen devil, whom she refers to as the "father of lies." She saw him in the Lutherans who were, in her opinion, destroying the churches, breaking the images of Christ and his saints, desecrating the

Blessed Sacrament, spreading false doctrine. But she also saw Satan within the institution of Catholicism, eroding the good name of the Church and thus making it more vulnerable to attacks by Protestants and pagans.

One day, when Teresa was forty-three, one of the sisters got the idea for a reform order of the Carmelites, one which would live a simple life in the spirit of the ancient hermits of Mount Carmel. Teresa was enthusiastic, and selected for this planned venture the guiding Rule of Saint Albert, a primitive monastic rule that required vows of poverty and chastity, in addition to long hours of silence, meditation, and manual labor. The reform group took the name of Discalced Carmelites, discalced meaning barefoot, although as Teresa grew older she became impatient with the barefoot rule and allowed sandals to be worn. "There is too much going barefoot," she remarked.

When Teresa took her idea for a reform group to her superiors, "people talked about us, laughed at us, and declared that the idea was ridiculous," she writes in her *Autobiography*. There was a good deal of envy among the existing Carmelite nuns, compounded with resentment because they took the reform project as a statement that there was a problem with the way they were carrying on. Teresa was reported to the Holy Inquisition; one nun even recommended that she be incarcerated for recalcitrance. Fortunately, after continuous pleading and planning, Teresa's project was vindicated.

Teresa founded Saint Joseph's, the first convent of the reform group, in 1562. In 1567 she set up another convent at Medina del Campo. Convents followed quickly at Malagón, Valladolid, Duruelo, Toledo, Pastrana, Salamanca, Alba de Tormes, Segovia, Beas, Seville, Villanueva de la Jara, Palencia, and Soria. Today Discalced

Carmelites have houses in several countries, including America and Japan.

The stories Teresa tells, and the stories told about her, are poignant and revealing. She paints a vivid picture of her first meeting with John of the Cross, to whom she took immediately, calling him "my little Seneca" for his depth of learning. At the Medina convent Teresa reports staying up late at night to watch in case the Lutherans showed up to steal the Blessed Sacrament; she had a window especially set up for this purpose. Teresa can be a severe administrator; she includes as a remedy for disobedient nuns a few blows "well laid on."

In general, though, she was compassionate and fun-loving. During Christmas she often accompanied nuns playing drum and pipes and making up verses and carols. To a scandalized nun who wondered aloud about trivialities Teresa remarked, "We need all this to make life livable." She also made allowances for the varied interests of her nuns; when the prioress of the convent penalized a nun for excessive reading, Teresa commuted the sentence with the observation, "Better a bookworm than a fool."

In 1582, at the age of sixty-seven, Teresa fell ill and passed away. She was canonized by Pope Gregory XV in 1622. In her *Autobiography* is preserved the precious memory of one of Catholicism's most divine yet human creatures.

S • I • X

ignatius of loyola's

spiritual exercises

SAINT Ignatius of Loyola, founder of the order known as the Society of Jesus, helped spearhead the Catholic Counter-Reformation of the sixteenth and seventeenth centuries. His *Spiritual Exercises* was written early in this gallant adventurer's life; intended as a manual for secluded retreat, it nevertheless became a powerful inspirational weapon for Jesuit priests venturing deep into Protestant territory, defending the Catholic faith against all ecclesiastical slander. The great strength of the *Exercises*, which was the great strength of the Jesuits for hundreds of years, is that it brings together spiritual depth and intellectual rigor in matchless combination. This fusion of the domains of faith and reason, of soul and mind, was simply too much for the Reformers, who feared the Jesuits as much as they feared marauding Turks or Saracens. It was not uncommon for a Lutheran or Calvinist pastor to hastily pack up and leave town upon hearing that a Jesuit, armed with the Bible and the *Spiritual Exercises*, was arriving to debate him.

Born in 1491, Ignatius of Loyola's original name was Iñigo López de Loyola; later he would change it to Ignatius. His family was of Basque descent, and affluent;

town records show that they owned four homes and estates, a country homestead, two blacksmith shops, meadows and orchards, and one water mill. Ignatius was raised in the Spanish tradition of strong allegiance to Catholic doctrine but relative laxity in moral observance.

Ignatius spent his adolescent years as a page to Juan Velázquez de Cuéllar, a nobleman and confidant of King Ferdinand. An earlier biographer describes Ignatius as "lively and trim," fond of "court dress and good living," and enamored by tales of "knight errantry and valor." In his own diaries Ignatius speaks of his desire to win fame, perhaps in some great battle. This martial strain in Ignatius would stay with him all his life; later Jesuits would say of his irrevocable decisions, "He has driven in the nail." Ignatius was ever a firm and perhaps recalcitrant man.

In 1517, at the age of twenty-six, Ignatius became a gentleman in the service of the viceroy of Navarre, where he inhaled the aroma of war. In 1520 he participated in the expedition that extinguished riots in the towns of the Castile. In 1521 he organized security in the Guipúzcoa area, where there was enormous civil division and strife. Little did the hotheaded soldier know that, about the same time, an obscure theologian named Martin Luther was publishing and promulgating his ninety-five theses at Wittenberg and elsewhere in Germany.

In 1521, during a battle resisting the French occupation of Navarre, Ignatius was badly wounded by a cannon ball which passed between his legs, shattering the right one and damaging the other. Doctors found their treatments to little avail, so they brought in clergy to administer to Ignatius the last rites. But just as he was given up for dead, Ignatius made an unexpected recovery. It was this time of illness and repose that enabled Ignatius to come to terms with the fate of his soul. He had asked for books of chivalry to read, but his family could only find around the house a number of religious books. Ignatius was deeply influenced by *Vita Christi*, a life of Christ written by a Carthusian monk, and a Spanish version of the popular sixteenth-century manual on the lives of the saints. His attitude toward the saints was exactly the one he might have entertained had he been reading about Sir Lancelot or King Arthur. "Saint Francis did this? Then I must do it." So Ignatius describes his response to the spiritual lives that excited his imagination.

Ironically in the very year that Ignatius was making his way into the faith, Martin Luther was making his way out of it. On January 3, 1521, Luther was excommunicated at the Diet of Worms. Meanwhile Ignatius was resolving to undertake a pilgrimage to Jerusalem and commit himself to a holy life patterned on the saints he had read about. In confirmation of these resolutions, Ignatius reports that he experienced a "visitation," in which he saw the likeness of the Virgin Mary and Child Jesus; he awoke with a deep understanding of the magnitude of his sins, and a conviction to avoid the temptation of the flesh.

Ignatius' family, eager that he assume his duties as head of the ancestral manor, implored him not to undertake rash voyages based on nocturnal visions. But in February of 1522, with backpacks and a mule, Ignatius set out for Jerusalem. He stopped at Montserrat, where he located a French Benedictine monk and confessed the transgressions of his whole life. It was the feast of the Annunciation of Mary, so Ignatius set aside his rich garments and donated them to a roadside tramp; he put on a pilgrim's tunic and began a spiritual retreat.

From there Ignatius went on to Manresa, where he would spend almost a year. This period of his life was characterized by troubling interior scruples, which Ignatius desperately struggled to vanquish. He refused to eat meat and drink wine. He allowed his hair to grow long. In a touch of overkill, perhaps, he refused to trim his fingernails. He resolved to pray for seven hours a day. He would only speak of spiritual matters to those he met. Ignatius describes one temptation, where the devil taunted him, "How can you bear this life for the remaining seventy years of your life?" Ignatius was stung and depressed, but found reserves to respond, "Wretched being, can you promise me a single hour of life?" Ignatius' doubts persisted, however, until one day, during prayer and meditation, he felt an infusion of divine grace that purged his soul. No longer did he continue to agonize over sins that he had forgotten to confess. Ignatius felt spiritually whole.

"It was no vision that was granted me, but an understanding of many things — of the mind, of faith, of human knowledge — and in so clear a light that all seemed renewed from top to bottom," Ignatius says. A new man emerged from the cave of Manresa. "The pilgrim," he says, referring to himself, "saw such and such a thing in his soul, then such and such another, deciding that it was useful; and so, in the belief that he would be helping others, he wrote a book." The experience of Manresa would result in the first draft of the *Spiritual Exercises*.

The little book was to serve a function akin to Benedict's famous *Rule*. It was to be a manual for Christians on retreat — a mechanism for them to bring their soul into communion with God. Although written in a didactic and occasionally elliptical style, Ignatius filled the *Exercises* with practical wisdom, no doubt drawn from his personal experience and development. He also understood that diverse paths can lead to heaven; his *Exercises* is a supple and malleable text, which spiritual instructors are told to adapt to the particular circumstances and makeup of the souls under their care. Ignatius continued to add and subtract from the *Exercises* in his later life; he did not view the text as literature but as a set of evolving guidelines for pragmatic implementation. Later these rules would comprise the spiritual regimen of Jesuits and other priests on several continents, not just in the seditious air of Germany and England but also in the exotic pagan environs of India and Indonesia and China and Africa.

The *Exercises* together compromise a surprisingly compact volume, a booklet barely a hundred pages long, a fraction of the length of the windy Protestant texts appearing one after another in that era. Ignatius, however, writes in lean and manly prose, eschewing ornamentation. He wrote in Castilian, the rugged dialect of the Basques. Punctuation was not his strong point, neither did he abstain from an occasional malapropism or obsolete word. But for all this his prose is forceful and pungent, unforgettably to the point.

The premise of Ignatius is that "man is neither an angel nor a brute beast," in Pascal's memorable phrase. Man occupies a middle position between rational perfection and slavery to the senses. Ignatius realizes that man is capable of reason; indeed it is reason that establishes him as man. Reason is corrupt, but it cannot be distrusted totally — otherwise it would be impossible even to establish that reason is corrupt. While man can understand through reason, though, he can only learn from habit and experience. Abstract recognition does not a convert make. Ignatius' *Exercises* are catered both to the mind and the senses, both to intellectual understanding and the cultivation of discipline. Ignatius does not eschew routinization because he knows that this is how man imbibes knowledge — not just into his head but into his whole being. Ultimately Ignatius stresses the importance of will, because it controls both mind and feelings. Through organized procedure, including the record of lapses and progress in charts and graphs, Ignatius provides the will with a compass to direct the haphazard and unpredictable forces of man's nature toward holiness.

The ostensible purpose of the *Exercises* is for the Christian to discover God's will for the disposition of his life: Should he, for example, enter the religious life or into marriage? Ignatius knew the magnetic pull of secular motives for both the clerical and married vocations. For instance, one might seek the priesthood because of confusion about one's identity, fear about secular responsibilities, or merely the desire to have one's material needs cared for. Similarly one might pursue marriage purely to satisfy lust, or to have the dishes washed regularly at home. Ignatius firmly believed that these decisions should be oriented toward the divine will. God wants to help us, he says, to "order our life without making decisions through some affections which are disordered." The *Exercises* prepares the soul for a direct communication with God about this most important project that he has for our lives.

More generally, however, the book is aimed at bringing Christians into a better appreciation for how they can best serve God through an imitation of Christ and an acceptance of his graces. Ignatius freely admits that this is no dilettante enterprise; it is for Christians who truly love God and are willing to dedicate their lives to him. This is Catholic elitism, to be sure, but it is a privilege that is open to all, including — perhaps especially — the poor; Ignatius would ever rebuke Christians who valued the honors of birth above spiritual riches, and he established the vow of poverty as an essential requirement for the new order that he would found, the Jesuits.

"Just as strolling, walking or running are bodily exercises, so spiritual exercises are methods of preparing and disposing the soul to free itself of all inordinate attachments . . . to seek and discover the divine will . . . and insure the salvation of the soul." So this great book begins, then proceeds to outline a regimen of prayer, contemplation, and even diet for four successive weeks. The demands on the retreatant grow increasingly rigorous, and Ignatius is careful to caution spiritual directors against automatic advance. Christians, he specifies, must be kept at a level corresponding to their interior development. Thus the four weeks of the *Exercises* need not correspond to calendar weeks; rather they refer to metaphysical periods or brackets of time, much as the "seven days" of Genesis, the first book of the Bible, alludes to the intervals of creation.

The principles underlying the entire project are specified right away. "Man is created to praise, revere and serve God, and by this means to save his soul. All other things on the face of the earth are created for man to help him fulfill the end for which he is created. From this it follows that man is to use these things to the extent that they will help him attain his end. Likewise, he must rid himself of them insofar as they prevent him from attaining it."

We begin the retreat with a general examination of conscience. We have three kinds of thoughts, Ignatius says: those which come from ourselves, those which come from God, and those which come from the devil.

The two latter kinds of thought eventually merge with the first, in that we must ultimately decide whether exterior impulses are either accepted or rejected. Temptation is not a sin, of course, but acquiescence in temptation is sinful. Immediately we should repel all thoughts of mortal sin from our mind, Ignatius recommends. Even if we do, he adds, we must be sure to be prompt and decisive because we are guilty of venial sin if we procrastinate, thus enjoying the sensual pleasure of temptation. We sin mortally, by contrast, if we put the temptation into action or willfully intend to at some later time.

Throughout our reflections we should ask God to duplicate, in us, the experience that Christ had during that particular phase of our study. For instance, "If the contemplation is on the resurrection, I shall ask for joy with Christ rejoicing; if it is on the passion, I shall ask for pain, tears and suffering." In the first phase we ask for "shame and confusion," a prelude to understanding "how many souls have been damned for a single mortal sin, and how often I have deserved to be damned eternally for the many sins I have committed."

In order to comprehend our own sins, we should begin by considering the sin committed by Lucifer, that first angel who rebelled against God through pride and hubris. Then, Ignatius recommends, we dwell on the sin of Adam and Eve, who disobeyed God's edict about the tree of good and evil. Finally we imagine the sins of other men and women, including our own, thinking of them in conjunction with the image of Christ on the cross, writhing and bleeding because of what we did to him. We close this meditation with a resolution to accept Christ's saving grace and to amend our lives in the future.

Ignatius now bids us, in a separate exercise, to come to terms with hell. Again, he recommends a sequential awareness beginning with us imagining "the length, breadth and depth of hell." We should, for example, "imagine the great fires, and the souls enveloped in bodies of fire." We should "hear the wailing, the screaming, the cries and blasphemies against Christ." We should "smell the smoke, the brimstone, the corruption and rottenness." We should "taste bitter things, as tears, sadness and remorse of conscience." We should virtually "touch to feel how the flames surround and burn souls."

Throughout the *Exercises* Ignatius recommends fasting or regulation of diet. By this he does not mean skipping those sumptuous desserts or going easy on the roast beef. "It will be noted," he says, "that when we deny ourselves what is superfluous, it is not penance but temperance. It is penance when we deny ourselves what is proper for us to have, and the more we deny ourselves the greater and better is the penance, provided we do not harm ourselves." Penance also includes "sensible pain" by which Ignatius means "wearing hairshirts, cords or iron chains on the body," even scouring oneself with "light cords" so as to "cause pain but not illness." The objective is to make our lower inclinations subject to our higher ones, "to make sensuality subject to reason," in Ignatius' words. Also to give us some small indication of the indescribable agony Christ suffered on Calvary to atone for the sins of the world.

From a meditation of our own sins we proceed to an appreciation of Christ. We imagine in our mind a human king, adorned with all the robes and regalia of a Peter the Great, or Louis XIV. Do not think of a despot, Ignatius warns, but a benevolent and splendid monarch — unrivaled in human excellence. Then magnify this vision and apply it to Christ, the King of Heaven. In the next set of exercises, we go — scene by scene — through Christ's birth and life: the angel Gabriel appearing to our Lady, the Nativity, Christ among wise men, and so on. In each case we seek to relive Christ's experience, to be there, as it were. For instance, visualizing baby Jesus in the manger, "I will become a poor, miserable, and unworthy slave looking upon him, contemplating him, and ministering his needs, as though I were present." Going through the exercises, we realize by now, is a constant effort in empathy — putting ourselves in other places, putting ourselves in the place of others.

In his famous discussion of the Two Standards, Ignatius asks us to experience the presence of the evil force and the good force in human affairs. First, "imagine how the evil chieftain of all the enemy is seated at the center of the vast plain of Babylon, on a great throne of fire and smoke — a horrible and terrible sight to behold." We watch him "call together countless demons, see how he scatters them . . . throughout the whole world, missing no province, no place, no state of life, nor even any single person." To understand his determination, we listen to the harangue that he delivers to them, spurring them on to ensnare men and bind them in chains. Riches, honor, and pride are his bait; "from these three steps Satan leads on to all other vices."

We contrast this with an experience of Christ, who "takes his stand in a lowly place, in that plain of Jerusalem." He, too, chooses deputies called Apostles, disciples, and missionaries, and sends them far and wide to spread the sacred doctrine. Christ charges his followers to seek virtues opposite to the vices promoted by his deadly adversary: "poverty as opposed to riches, humility as opposed to pride, scorn or contempt as opposed to worldly honor." Such self-understanding and self-abnegation lead men to all other virtues.

Ignatius' discussion of the Two Standards is the most martial section of the book. Ignatius presents God and Satan as commanding two hostile armies. We imagine them poised on the two sides of a river, rousing their battalions to action. Here strict discipline is demanded by Ignatius, because a terrible war is about to be waged whose issue is nothing less than the future of the soul for all eternity. The term "spiritual exercises" is here understood in a very literal military sense: that of equipping and preparing for battle.

Ignatius now introduces his Three Modes of Humility, the essential prerequisite to making a sound choice for the future of one's life. The initial step is to "humble and abase myself as much as possible for me, in order that I may obey in all things the law of God our Lord." This requires us to accept that it would be worse for us to commit a single mortal sin than to enjoy and control all the material pleasures that the world has to proffer. The second mode of humility, superior to the first, requires that "I neither desire nor even prefer to have riches than dishonor, to have a long life rather than a short one." I seek only the "opportunity to serve God, and save my soul." Total indifference to the temptations of the flesh is the goal here; it is not that worldly goods are evil, rather for us they become, at this point, irrelevant. Finally, in the third and "most perfect" phase of humility, "I desire and choose poverty with Christ rather than riches, in order to be like Christ. . . . I choose reproaches with Christ suffering rather than honor. . . . I am willing to be considered to be worthless and a fool for Christ rather than to be esteemed as wise and prudent." All actions, in other words, are oriented toward the greater glory of God.

It is at this point that we first fully understand Ignatius' famous words: "What does it profit a man if he gain the whole world but suffer the loss of his soul?" These are the words that have echoed on the lips of Jesuits on five continents, and contributed to the devotion of countless men to a life of service to God. Once we appreciate the stakes involved, we are ready to think about how we want to spend the rest of our lives.

In making a vocational choice, Ignatius says, "I must not shape or draw the end to the means, but the means to an end." For instance, we should not marry and then think about how we can serve God in the married state. The reason is that marriage is a means, not an end. We should marry if that is the way God wants us to serve him. Individuals who make their own choices and then try to steer religion around them, Ignatius says, "do not go straight to God but want God to come straight to them through their inordinate attachments." Whether we end up in the clerical or lay life, whether we marry or remain single, in all things we should seek God's will for us. What follows is an incisive psychological process to determine this.

Ignatius knows that God does not communicate himself through wild epiphanies on a regular basis. He also knows how difficult it is for us humans to distinguish between spiritual experience and hallucination. He knows the temptations and risks that come with us aspiring to visions, prophecies, and miracles. So often Christians ascribe to divine instruction courses of action that they, for very human reasons, intend to undertake.

Here are a few steps Ignatius suggests. "I must ask God to design to move my will and to reveal to my spirit what I should do." In addition, "I use my reason to weigh the many advantages and benefits that would accrue to me if I held the proposed office solely for the praise of God and the salvation of my soul." If the choice appears unclear or difficult, "I consider some man that I have never seen or known, and in whom I see complete perfection. I consider what I would tell him to do . . . and act in like manner myself, keeping the rule that I have proposed for another." Further, "I consider that if I were at the point of death, what form and procedure would I wish to have observed in making this present choice?" Through these guidelines, Ignatius says, we can come to a richer understanding of God's will for us. Once we have reached a tentative judgment, we should offer it to God in prayer, so that he may confirm it through the solace and peace that come from direct communication with him.

We pray, "Take, O Lord, and receive all my liberty, my memory, my understanding, and my entire will, all that I have and possess. Thou hast given all to me; to Thee, O Lord, I return it. All is Thine; dispose of it according to Thy will. Give me Thy love and Thy grace, for this is enough for me."

The rest of the *Exercises* focuses on prayer and meditation on passages from Scripture. We go through the Ten Commandments, considering each one in all its implications, remembering how we may have violated each. We consider the seven capital sins and their reciprocal virtues. We resolve to avoid the sins and strive for the goodness that comes through this. We take prayers such as the Our Father, the Apostles' Creed, the Hail Mary, and the Hail Holy Queen, ruminating on each word of each prayer. For instance, with the Our Father, Ignatius recommends that we spend an hour considering the word "father," reflecting upon its various meanings and comparisons. In what sense, for instance, is God like our human father? What does our father do for us? What obligations do we accrue as children? What about Saint

Joseph, Jesus' earthly father? What was his reaction to the plan for Jesus outlined to his wife by God, the heavenly Father? In like measure, we consider every single word of the prayer.

The *Exercises* is, in these advanced states, an extremely demanding rulebook for spiritually mature souls. Some commentators have observed that it is not proper fare for an annual retreat; rather it is an experience for a lifetime. If conducted in the right manner, one emerges in close communion with God, equipped with enough graces and resolve to dispel the wiles of Satan.

Despite the rigors of the *Exercises*, Ignatius throughout emphasizes the flexibility of his spiritual regimen. He is interested in results, not process. Thus he gladly subordinates procedure to the attainment of the goals he seeks. In later years the adaptability of the order Ignatius founded, the Jesuits, would be their great strength, because it would enable them to distill the principles of the Catholic faith in diverse civilizations in Asia and Africa, preserving doctrines while amending non-essential forms to suit local customs and practices. At the same time flexibility and adaptability, when pursued in unrestrained manner, can lead to all manner of falsehoods and surrender of truth — this was a pit into which Ignatius never let himself fall.

Ignatius, in his concluding sections, considers the continuing threat to souls posed by the devil. "The enemy acts like a woman in that he is weak in the presence of strength, but strong if he has his will. For as it is the nature of a woman in a quarrel with a man to lose courage and take to flight when the man makes a show of strength and determination, in like manner, if the man loses courage and begins to flee, the anger, vindictiveness and rage of the woman become great beyond all bounds. In the same manner it is the nature of our enemy to become powerless, lose courage and take to flight as soon as a person who is following the spiritual life stands courageously against his temptation." No doubt there are some who would dismiss this analogy as hopelessly sexist and antiquated; but many of us instead wonder how Ignatius, who devoted himself to the celibate life, would possibly understand such things about men and women so clearly.

"The enemy also behaves like a false lover who wishes to remain hidden and does not want to be revealed," Ignatius says. "For when this deceitful man pays court, with evil intent, to the daughter of some good father or a wife of a good husband, he wants his words and suggestions to be kept secret. He is greatly displeased if the girl reveals to her father, or the wife to her husband, his deceitful words and depraved intentions, for he then clearly sees that his plans cannot succeed. In like manner, when the enemy of our human nature tempts a just soul with his wiles and deceits, he wishes and desires that they be received and kept in secret. When they are revealed to a confessor or some other spiritual person who understands his evil designs, the enemy is greatly displeased for he knows that he cannot succeed."

A third comparison. "The enemy's behavior is like that of a military leader who wishes to conquer and plunder the object of his desires. Just as the commander of an army pitches his camp, studies the strength and defenses of a fortress, and then attacks on its weakest side, in like manner the enemy of our human nature studies from all sides our theological, cardinal and moral virtues. Wherever he finds us weakest . . . he attacks and takes us by storm."

Throughout our spiritual exercise, Ignatius knows, it

is not just Christ but also the evil spirit who is at work. How are we to distinguish between these noncorporal forces? Further, how do we know whether our soul is in communion with one or the other? Ignatius writes, "In those who are making progress, the action of the good angel is gentle, light and sweet, as a drop of water entering a sponge. The action of the evil spirit is sharp, noisy and disturbing, like a stone falling upon a rock." The reason is that our soul reacts pleasantly or unpleasantly depending on whether the spirit it encounters is harmonious with its own disposition or incongruent with it.

A final rule given us by Ignatius is one that is perhaps germane to the Church today. "Putting aside all private judgement, we should keep our minds prepared and ready to obey promptly and in all things the true spouse of Christ, our Holy Mother the hierarchical Church." Ignatius vaunts Scripture, on which Church teaching is based; he vaunts the pronouncements of the pope and the sacred councils. He urges all Christians "to praise all the precepts of the Church, holding ourselves ready at all times to find reasons for their defense, and never offending against them." When controversial doctrines are being discussed — Ignatius thinks of the issue of grace versus good works, or free will versus predestination — we should speak cautiously, in scrupulous harmony with Catholic teaching. There are no exceptions to this rule. "If we wish to be sure that we are right in all things, we should always be ready to accept this principle: I will believe that the white I see is black, if the hierarchical Church so defines it."

One does not find, in the *Exercises*, the lofty soaring of mystical experience that one finds in Teresa of Ávila or John of the Cross. Ignatius is not the saint of the high snows, but the saint of service on the ground. Throughout, his goal was dedication, commitment, and conversion. Thus it is no surprise that he was able to recruit armies of soldiers for Christ who crossed the oceans and scaled the hills to confront, combat, and evangelize unbelievers and heretics.

In his famous letter on the Virtue of Obedience, issued in 1533, Ignatius writes to Jesuits in Portugal: "We may easily suffer ourselves to be surpassed by other Religious Orders in fasting, watching and other austerities of diet and clothing, which they practice according to their rule, but in true and perfect obedience, and in the abnegation of our will and judgement, I greatly desire, most dear brethren, that those who serve God in this Society should be conspicuous."

It is just and appropriate that the *Exercises* should end on a note of total self-surrender and obedience. This, after all, is the great virtue of the soldier; he commits his life to a cause larger than himself, willing to follow his superiors even when their orders run counter to his intuition or wisdom. Giving up liberty of thought is difficult, Ignatius knows, but to give it up willingly and joyfully, and the conviction that one is actually better for this surrender — that is the mark of a true Christian soldier. That is the mark of a Jesuit.

Through obedience and dedication Ignatius hoped to win back the lost divisions of the Church. But no one who reads the *Exercises* or any of Ignatius' works will find them defensive or negative in tone. They are not prayers or pleas against an enemy; rather, they are enterprises of mind and soul undertaken for God. The purpose of Ignatius' disciplinary canon is primarily to strengthen men in their relationship with Christ, only secondarily and through persuasion of example to collapse the position of adversaries.

If readers are surprised by the mystic flavor of the *Exercises*, influenced perhaps by the stereotype of the Jesuits as great rationalists, they should understand that all the towering personalities of Catholic thought have shown a powerful mystical side — Aquinas and Ignatius are no exception. It is wrong to think of Protestant mysticism providing a needed antidote to Catholic rationalism; where, among Protestants, can be found those whose mysticism soared as high as that of John of the Cross, Teresa of Ávila, and yes, Ignatius of Loyola?

Ignatius' mysticism, however, is different in character from that of Thomas à Kempis, whose *Imitation of Christ*, written in the fifteenth century, proposes isolation from the world of men — retirement into the cocoon of personal interaction with God — as a way of coping with the problems of the world and the institution of the Church. Ignatius, rather, eschews the monastic enclosure for a form of spirituality that is extroverted, outward-reaching, even adventurous. Faith in Ignatius' model is not a protective blanket but a helmet — donned to keep the Christian whole in the face of enemy artillery. Ignatius has more in common with the tradition of the crusaders than with the tradition of Thomas à Kempis or Benedict.

Innumerable saints, from Francis Xavier to Alphonsus Liguori to Charles Borromeo to Vincent de Paul, found the *Exercises* to be invaluable to their effort to evangelize the Catholic faith in a difficult time. Both Jesuits and others employed it as a tool of spiritual regeneration both within the continent of Europe and abroad. Persuasion and holiness were the resources used to convert pagans and "our separated brethren," to use Jesuit Peter Canisius' term for Protestants.

When Ignatius took a handful of devout friends to the

mountain of Montmarte on August 15, 1534, they took all implicit vows of poverty, chastity, and obedience. Later, these vows, together with a commitment to evangelization and mission, would characterize the new order of the Jesuits. The *Exercises* were routinely given by the Society of Jesus not just in Catholic countries (such as France, Italy, and Spain) but also in Germany and England, where the Jesuits invaded in force, founding schools, colleges, and seminaries. For the Jesuits, Ignatius stressed "modesty and Christian charity" in all their efforts, a "love of good works," and "arguments of speech, arguments of deed, arguments of blood."

Ignatius was to spend the last part of his life administering the flourishing Jesuit order. In 1541 Ignatius completed his Constitutions of the Society, a spiritual and organizational classic in itself, which guides the Jesuits to this day. Ignatius died on July 31, 1556. He was beatified a little over fifty years later, in 1609. In 1622 he was canonized.

robert bellarmine's

controversies

URING the tempestuous time of the rise of Protestantism following the Reformation, the Catholic Church needed the stouthearted souls who would defend the faith against calumnies and distortions, while at the same time militating for needed reform. Saint Ignatius of Loyola spearheaded the spiritual revival with his founding of the Jesuit order. The Jesuits combined deep faith with ordered and combative intellect and, in the brilliance and determination of their efforts, fomented fear and confusion in the Lutheran and Calvinist camps. One of the most formidable Jesuit polemicists for Catholicism was Saint Robert Bellarmine, whose *Controversies* profoundly influenced Church thinking for more than two hundred years. Somehow the faith has managed to raise great apologists during times of crisis — Saint Augustine during the fall of Rome, Saint Thomas during the Aristotelian revival; Bellarmine helped rescue the faith during the Protestant siege of the fifteenth, sixteenth, and seventeenth centuries, meeting the theological challenge of the reformers and guiding Catholicism to a new vigor and confidence in the future.

In the twentieth century Catholicism faces, in North

and South America, a renewed Protestant evangelical threat, generated by the erosion of moral values in our society and the promise of fundamentalist denominations to return to scriptural basics. Bellarmine's arguments, which have hibernated for some time now, thus arise with an urgency and clarity that contemporary Catholics would do well to understand. Here, after all, is a profound and thorough discussion of "Bible only" Christianity, of papal infallibility, of sacraments such as confession and the Eucharist, of the role of "works" in contributing to salvation. It makes lengthy and often technical reading, but the reader who makes the effort is amply compensated. He emerges with a fortified comprehension of Catholic doctrine.

Robert Bellarmine was born on the feast of Saint Francis of Assisi, October 4, 1542, in the little town of Montepulciano near Tuscany in Italy. His mother, Cynthia, attended a retreat patterned on the *Spiritual Exercises* of Ignatius; as a result, she was determined to send all of her five sons into the Society of Jesus. Robert attended the local grammar school where he studied Latin, ancient Greek, and Roman history, developing a particular affinity for Cicero and Virgil. In his childhood, he remembered the enthusiasm of Italian Catholics when Cardinal Marcello Cervini in 1555 was named Pope Marcellus II, because everyone was familiar with nepotism and abuses that had crept into the Church, and Marcellus was a dedicated reformer. Unfortunately this pope fell ill and died only three weeks after his election; the promise of reform was extinguished; the Protestant critique gained momentum.

Robert Bellarmine was a sickly child, whose lungs frequently developed this ailment or that. He was just about to enter medical school, perhaps because he wanted to understand his own failing constitution, when the Jesuits opened an academy in Montepulciano. His mother promptly transferred him there, at the age of fifteen; Robert, already a devout and prayerful Catholic, was pleased to attend. Immediately he developed a passion for Aristotle and the great philosopher's reasoning grounded in a commonsense understanding of nature. Unfortunately Robert would pick up some dubious Aristotelian notions about astronomy as well. In one of his early books he writes, "I was desirous of learning what space of time the sun would take in setting. At the beginning of its setting I began to recite the Psalm *Miserere Mei Deus*, and I had scarce read it twice through when the whole sun had set. So in that short space of time the sun must traverse in its course a distance of much greater than seven thousand miles." Such amateur theorizing would later lead Bellarmine to sympathize with the Vatican's chastisement of Galileo for promulgating supposedly unscriptural scientific hypotheses. But we can be thankful that Bellarmine's lifework was devoted to the largely unrelated field of theology, where his competence was unrivaled in his time and his ideas infinitely more subtle and convincing.

In 1563 Robert was sent to his native environs of Tuscany because his Jesuit preparation at Rome was having an adverse effect on his health. Already equipping himself for Jesuit vows of poverty and hardship, he traveled the two-hundred-mile journey on foot. The Italian air proved good for him, and he quickly recuperated. He was always extremely studious; as his memory developed, his superiors found that he could remember a Latin sermon of more than an hour's length by reading it over once. Robert was soon sent off to Mondovi in Piedmont, then part of the duchy of Savoy, for further studies. This resulted in another lengthy journey during which the poor seminarian was accused of stealing a purse by a foolish innkeeper; at another place his hostess embarrassed him by claiming him as the long-lost husband of her daughter. Later Bellarmine would wryly treat these experiences in his sermons.

Robert's preaching skills were honed at Mondovi, although he did not neglect mundane duties such as daily teaching, janitorial work, and readings to elderly Fathers in the evenings. He did a short stint at Padua and Genoa, where the Jesuit provincial Adorno engaged him in scholastic disputations. Attacks on Aristotle and Aquinas were hurled unexpectedly at the young prodigy, and he was expected to parry and rebut. All were struck by his eloquence, modesty, and courtesy, and the decision was made to send him to Louvain University in Belgium, a node center in the Catholic resistance against Protestant attack and subversion.

In 1570, the year of his ordination, Bellarmine was named the first Jesuit professor at Louvain. He would spend seven years there, cultivating habits of spiritual discipline, and intellectual fairness and proficiency, that would propel him to the summit of Catholic apologetics. Even in his early lecture notes we see hints of this; when he quotes Saint Augustine, for instance, he gives not two or three references but no less than fifteen, all direct quotes from the great Father's prolific works.

We also see vestiges of Bellarmine's spiritual courage; in a sermon addressed to ministers he says, "Preachers who are anxious to do their duty must not suffer themselves to be frightened away from wholesome teaching, merely because by delivering it they make enemies among their flock. He is but a sad and sorry evangelist who seeks his own and not God's glory, and desires to be loved and praised by the people, instead of bending all his energies to make God loved and praised by them. . . . Suppose a devoted husband, who is on a journey, sends his wife some little gift or token by a messenger, and the fellow uses it to ingratiate himself with the lady, would we not rightly account him a scoundrel and an adulterer at heart? Tell me now, if Christ the heavenly spouse of the holy Church sends her a message through a preacher, and he instead of delivering it faithfully, tries to appear a grand fellow on account of his commission, and uses the very Scriptures to show off his own eloquence and win the world's applause — tell me, I say, what better is he in the eyes of God than the adulterer?"

Louvain taught Bellarmine that the Protestant challenge, though misguided, was serious and far-reaching; it would not do to dismiss or distort the arguments of Reformers, as many priests were prone to do. Bellarmine followed Thomas Aquinas's example in stating, as forcibly as possible, the claims of his adversaries, and then systematically answering them with copious references to Scripture, the patristic writings, and the documents of the Church tradition. He was so fair to his opponents that some Catholics feared he was helping them out with arguments that hadn't occurred to them; the Hungarian prelate Stephen Arator complains, "Learned men out in central Europe consider that the *Controversies* have done more harm than good to the Church. Instead of depriving the heretics of their weapons, they do but supply them with new ones. Calvinists and Lutherans would never have the wit to think out so many and such excellent arguments for their sects as they may now find in Bellarmine. The result is that his volumes are being cited by Protestants more than Catholics."

This was a complaint that was actually an unintended compliment. Bellarmine rebutted Arator with the same fairness and effectiveness that he demonstrated against the Protestants. Should Catholics argue like that Spanish friar Orantes, "whose work makes all educated Catholics in France and Germany weep, and all the heretics hilarious, because their author, after answering a few petty arguments of Calvin, pretends that the gentleman has nothing better to say for himself"? Should those erudite Catholic bishops who reprinted in their pamphlets both Luther's claims and their own rebuttals be censured for giving space to the enemy? "If I had brought forward the arguments of Protestants and Catholics and let the two sets stand without further remark, there would be something to what my censor says," Bellarmine writes. "But since I have refuted the heretical and strengthened the Catholic position, what room is there for cavil? Had I not produced all the arguments I could discover on their side, the heretics would say that the ones I omitted were unanswerable." Finally Bellarmine points out that a number of cardinals and popes have specifically requested that he answer "all conceivable difficulties" raised by the reformers. The real vindication of Bellarmine comes from the consternation and demoralization he caused all his life among not just Protestants but also freethinkers and Jews, who found their positions being deflated and undermined, and the renewed confidence and optimism generated among Catholics across the Continent for generations to come.

Bellarmine always distinguished between small causes and large ones. Once he listened to finely woven conundrums and sighed, "Would it not be better to wait for the solution until we get to heaven?" On the other hand larger challenges could not wait. In 1559 Luther's most enthusiastic and competent disciple, Mathias Francowitz, published the first volume of his *Centuries of Magdeburg* under the alias Flaccius Illyricus. The study purported to prove that the Catholic Church was not legitimately descended from the Apostles, its family tree was faked, and Protestantism was, in fact, the true successor of early Christianity. Volume after volume of this study appeared between 1559 and 1574, alarming Catholic scholars very greatly. Stanislaus Hosius, the papal legate, considered the *Centuries* to be "the most pernicious work ever written," and the pope urged Jesuit historians to refute the Centuriators.

Bellarmine was transferred to the chair of controversial theology at the Roman College (now called the Gregorian University) where he prepared to issue his grand answer. "Today, gentlemen, we approach those questions which are at issue between the Church of the living God and heir to rebellious and furtive sons. . . . Our concern will not be with little things that make no difference however they stand, nor with the subtleties of metaphysics which a man may ignore without being any worse for it, but with God, with Christ, with the Church, with the Sacraments, and with a multitude of other matters which pertain to the very foundations of our faith." At the relatively young age of thirty-four, this man was mounting a counteroffensive that would shake the foundations of the anti-papist edifice.

The *Controversies*, which emerged out of lectures Bellarmine delivered at the Roman College, were published in three volumes at Inglostat from 1586 to 1593. So powerful were they that, in six years, they enhanced his reputation enough to give him the red hat: he was made a cardinal. Because Bellarmine did not merely use the Neoplatonist or Aristotelian categories of early Christian thought, but rather integrated into his arguments the new reasoning of the humanist historians and thinkers, he caught many of his opponents, both Protestant and secular, off guard. With scholarship and deep piety, with rigor and grace, Cardinal Bellarmine massed the ranks of his arguments to confound and overwhelm his opponents. Post-Tridentine Catholicism would never be the same.

Bellarmine is sometimes criticized for not being original. He would take the charge as a compliment. First of all he was defending the one true faith established by Jesus Christ and articulated through the Bible and Church tradition; since the truth was laid down, to be original would depart from the truth. Certainly Bellarmine admitted that Catholic doctrine could develop, but only from the premises already contained in Scripture or existing tradition. At the Council of Trent the discriminating task of clarifying the precise contours of Catholic orthodoxy had been breathtakingly accomplished; Bellarmine's task was not further refinement or development but rather defense and preservation. He was to the Council of Trent what the Carolingian renaissance was to the early Church formulations: he took what was there, and did his best to preserve it with its best luster and brilliance.

The preface to the *Controversies* outlines their sweeping format. Bellarmine notes that Lucifer, "the enemy of the human race and the father of confusion," has from the earliest times attempted to sow dissension and lies within the body of Christ's chosen people. "He started in the earliest ages with an assault on the Creed, having for his allies such heretics as the Manicheans and Gnostics." These people tried to "overthrow belief in

God the Father." When that failed, in the third century the devil turned his attention to the second person of the Trinity, Christ. The Arian and Sabellian heretics challenged his divinity. "Next with Photius and his followers came the great attack on the Holy Ghost." Fortunately the Catholic Church rebuked all these initiatives, so from the year A.D. 1000 the devil has concentrated on the ninth and tenth articles of the Creed: "I believe in one holy Catholic and Apostolic Church, the communion of saints, the forgiveness of sins." Berengarians, Waldensians, Albigensians, Wycliffites, Lutherans, Zwinglians, Calvinists, and Anabaptists all united against these articles. Bellarmine proposes to explain how Christ is the "head and ruler" of his Church; how the pope is the "visible head" of that Church "laboring here on earth"; what instruments the earthly Church has devised to help its members reach salvation, among them the sacraments and relics; and, finally, the crucial question of how justification by grace is compatible with free will. All of these questions were contested by the Protestants with vehemence.

Bellarmine does not confine his criticism to the *Centuries of Magdeburg*; he deals with a wide spectrum of complaints and commentaries. He finds, for instance, in the Lutheran *Book of Concord* "six grave blunders and sixty-seven lies," which are all documented. Even silly Protestant accusations, such as one claiming that the pope is the Antichrist, Bellarmine takes seriously, devoting thirty thousand words to an argument that makes anyone holding that Protestant view feel very sheepish at the end.

Bellarmine also refutes a preposterous legend of "Pope Joan" that made its way into the Protestant press. This Joan was supposed to be a woman who was in the habit of dressing like a man. She arrived in Rome, impressed everyone with her refinement and learning, and was promptly named to the Sacred College of Cardinals, soon to become pope. In one particularly elaborate version of the tale she is forced to resign when she gives birth to a child. With a sense of bemused but patient scholarship, Bellarmine dismantles the nonsense of this legend and lays the matter to rest. Rumors that Bellarmine does not deign to refute include: that several Roman pontiffs used famous "Italian sauce" to poison their predecessors; that a certain Catholic convent of nuns was found to contain the heads of six thousand immolated children; that the Society of Jesus hires professional thieves and murderers to do its dirty business. Scholarship can chase the exotic imagination only so far.

The first volume of the *Controversies* appeared in 1586, with endorsements from Pope Sixtus V, Emperor Rudolph II, and the Republic of Venice. The second volume, published in 1588, was even more lavishly endowed with endorsements; it cited more than three hundred ecclesiastical writers and historians as it plunged into the heart of Protestant claims and criticisms. It took five more years for Bellarmine's final volume, treating grace and free will, to appear at a time when the justification controversy was dividing not just reformers but also Catholics.

Here is a sample of Bellarmine's argument on the question of whether Christ is truly present in the sacrament of the Eucharist. Bellarmine considers what Jesus says: "This is my body. This is my blood. . . . Do this in memory of me." He comments, "Surely laws and decrees ought to be promulgated in clear, precise, simple terms and not obscurely or ambiguously. Otherwise any man might plead ignorance and say: let the legislator speak plainly if he wants his law to be kept. Now what Christian ever doubted that our Lord in instituting this Sacrament gave orders and framed a law that it was to be renewed perpetually in his Church? That is the literal meaning of: do this in memory of me. Since, then, these words of Christ are the expression of a law or command, to read figures or metaphors into them is to make Almighty God the most imprudent and incompetent of legislators.

"A man's last will and testament should surely be drawn up in the straightforward speech of everyday life. No one but a madman, or one who desired to make trouble after his death, would employ metonymy in such a document. When a testator says, 'I leave my house to my son John,' does anyone understand his words to mean, 'I leave to my son John, not my house itself standing four-square, but a nice painted picture of it'? In the next place, suppose a prince promised you a hundred gold pieces, and in fulfillment of his word sent a beautiful sketch of the coins, I wonder what you would think of his liberality? And suppose that, when you complained, the donor said, 'Sir, your astonishment is out of place, as the painted crowns you received may very properly be considered true crowns by the figure of speech called metonymy.' Would not everybody feel that he was making fun of you and your picture?

"Now our Lord promised to give us his flesh and blood. The bread which I shall give you, he said, is my flesh for the life of the world. If you argue that the bread may be looked upon as a figure of his flesh, you are arguing like the prince, making a mockery of God's promises. A wonderful gift indeed that would be, in which Eternal Wisdom, Truth, Justice and Goodness deceived us, its helpless pensioners, and turned our dearest hopes to derision.

"That I may show you how just and righteous is the position we hold, let us suppose that the last day has come and our doctrine of the Eucharist turns out to be false and absurd. If our Lord asks us reproachfully, 'Why did ye believe thus of my Sacrament? Why did ye adore the host?' May we not safely answer Him, 'Lord, if we were wrong in this, it was you who deceived us. We heard your word, this is my body. Was it a crime for us to believe you? We were confirmed in our mistake by a multitude of signs and wonders which could only have had you for their author. Your Church with one voice cried out to us that we were right, and in believing as we did but followed in the footsteps of all your saints and holy ones.' "

On and on this commentary goes, adding brick and mortar to Catholic doctrine, slowly dismantling the Protestant structure even as it erects a beautiful new one in its place — all this with such precision and nuance that the reader stands mesmerized, naturally converted before he really knows what has taken place.

In two annuals of Christian doctrine, a brief catechism for children and a larger handbook for teachers, Bellarmine simplifies many of the propositions in his *Controversies*. Here is an abbreviated discussion of sacraments and relics:

> *Pupil:* Would you explain to me how it is that the honor which we give to saints and their relics and images is not contrary to the first commandment, for we appear to adore them and pray to them as we do to God?
>
> *Teacher:* Holy Church is the bride of God and has the Spirit of God for her guide. Consequently, there is no danger of her being de-

ceived or doing or permitting anything contrary to God's commandments. To answer the question, we honor and invoke the saints because they are friends of God, and can help us by their merits and prayers to him. But we do not account them gods, nor do our genuflections signify any such thing. A genuflection is not a mark of reverence peculiar to the service of God, for knees are bent also to persons of great dignity, such as kings, and in many places religious men kneel before their superiors. It is not strange, then, that we should show such reverence to the saints reigning with Christ in heaven since we show it to mortal men like ourselves, here on earth.

Pupil: Is it possible to say the same about images?

Teacher: Yes, because images of our Lord, our Lady, and the saints are not regarded by us as gods, but as mere representations which recall to our minds thoughts of those they represent. The honor which we pay them is not given because they are figures of wood, paper, stone or metal, or because they are beautifully colored and molded, but because they represent Christ, his Mother, or the saints. Knowing as we do that the images are dead, undiscerning things, we do not ask anything of them and pray before them only because they picture to our minds the heavenly beings whom we are really addressing.

Pupil: Why do we represent in pictures God the Father as an old man or the Holy Ghost as a dove when we know that these are spirits who have no bodies that can be painted as artists paint men?

Teacher: When God the Father is represented as an old man, the Holy Ghost as a dove, and angels as winged youths, this is not done because they are really like that. They are bodiless spirits, we all know. But we give them human and earthly forms because it was under such that they revealed themselves to men. God the Father appeared as an old man in a vision to the prophet Daniel. The Holy Ghost is shown as a dove because it was in that form that he appeared at the baptism of our Lord. The pictures and statues we make are not intended to show us things in themselves but rather the quality of things, or the effects they produce. For instance, the Holy Spirit is represented as a dove to signify the gifts of innocence, purity and holiness which he endows in our souls. Similarly, angels are given wings because we know that their heavenly strength and beauty never decline, and they are always on tiptoe to do God's bidding. Sometimes we even see them in white robes and sacred stoles, signifying their sinlessness and service of the divine majesty.

While Bellarmine is rigorous in his explanation and justification of doctrine, he understands that it is the animation of Christ's love and spirit that should underline all Catholic belief and practice. Writing of the virtue of charity in *Controversies* he observes, "Who is there in our illustrious home of learning who does not think daily as he goes to the schools of law, medicine, philosophy or theology, how best he may progress in this particular subject, and win at last his doctor's degree? The school of Christ is the school of charity. On the last day, when the great general examination takes place, there will be no questions at all on the text of Aristotle, the aphorisms of Hippocrates, or the paragraphs of Justinian. Charity will be the whole syllabus."

Further, Catholic truths are meant not just to be understood, accepted, and defended but most important must be internalized in our own lives. "We must not suffer it to be said that the most holy and living sacrament of Eucharist was instituted for us in vain," Bellarmine writes. "The wheaten bread which is the food of our bodies was not grown in the fields, reaped, ground and baked merely to be looked at, but to be eaten to sustain our life and strength. So too the bread of angels was not given to us solely for our veneration, but for our nourishment as well, that by partaking of it we may refresh and fortify our souls."

Why have Christian virtues diminished among us today? Why do our lives so little resemble those of the first Christians? Bellarmine poses questions that are equally germane to us in the twentieth century. "Is it not because, in the psalmist's words we have forgotten to eat our bread? They, on the contrary, learned from the Apostles to take this most profitable and life-giving food every day, and so they became strong, robust, energetic soldiers for Christ, ready and trim for every labor, and for the last heroic conflict of martyrdom. Let us then try to be like them here on earth, that we may deserve to be their comrades in heaven."

Bellarmine's treatment of the Catholic Church's practice of the sale of indulgences is too complicated to fully expound. Suffice it to say that he treated the subject fully and fairly, reluctant but unfailing in his criticism of the human failures of the institutional Church where warranted. "I shall say something first about the names indulgence and jubilee, and give a list of those who have written in defense of indulgence or against them," Bellarmine begins. "The next step will be an inquiry whether indulgences exist, and here two matters have to be discussed, namely the spiritual treasury of the Church, and the power of distributing what is contained in the treasury. Thirdly we shall investigate the precise nature of an indulgence, and here also two points have to be explored, to wit, whether an indulgence be simply the payment of a debt or rather a judicial absolution, and if so from what bond the release or acquittal is given. Fourthly we shall treat of the many forms and varieties of indulgences, and fifthly, of their utility and fruit. In the sixth place we shall inquire who can grant them, and for what reasons. Then, seventhly, we shall see by whom and under what conditions they may be gained, and finally, whether and how they can be applied for the benefit of the dead. That will end the first section. In the second, I shall expound, discuss and refute the contrary arguments of Luther, Calvin, and Chemnitz, who are our chief opponents in this matter, and also lay bare their lies, frauds and impostures."

Nevertheless it should not be assumed that Bellarmine was simply using his reservoir of knowledge to rationalize unjustifiable deeds. He condemns the routinization of indulgences because, he says, they undermine Church discipline if people think that they can easily have penance commuted by a gift or donation to the Church. "Consider, I pray you," Bellarmine argues, "whether there is any proportion between these two things: attendance at a single Mass and deliverance from a hundred years of the most rigorous chastisement which the justice of God can inflict." Bellarmine points out that the practice of indulgences is relatively recent, being unknown in the early Church. He is pleased that the current pope grants them "only under many restrictions and for a limited time." If it were up to Bellarmine, he concludes, "none would be granted except little ones." The reason? "Indulgences cost our Lord his precious blood so they ought to be begged for with reluctance and pressing need." But Bellarmine does not deny that, in principle, the Church has the power through Christ to forgive sins. We become a bit more sympathetic, not just in principle but also in practice, when we discover that priests were handing out penances that included wearing sackcloth for months or abstaining from sexual relations with a spouse for several years. Indulgences, in these circumstances, amounted to a little more than an expression of Christian compassion to reduce the burden on the afflicted.

In his *Controversies* Bellarmine propounded a fascinating argument restricting the earthly power of the Catholic pope. The pontiff has supreme spiritual authority, but the temporal ruler, who is also appointed by God, has control of the earthly domain, the realm of Caesar. The pope's earthly jurisdiction is restricted to those lands that he himself owns. He is only justified in intervening in secular powers when they directly injure the spiritual interests of the faithful; in such limited cases, Bellarmine concedes to the Holy See the power even to depose kings and exonerate their subjects from an obligation to obey them. Pope Sixtus V was very displeased by Bellarmine's caveats about his temporal authority, even going to the extreme of listing the first volume of *Controversies* on the Index of Forbidden Books. He died, however, before the Index was published and his successor prudently removed Bellarmine's name from the unfortunate catalog of dissenters and infidels.

Bellarmine's argument has assumed contemporary interest in these days of separation of Church and State. His critics maintained that Christ, being God, naturally possessed both spiritual and temporal jurisdiction on earth — who would deny this? The pope is the vicar and lieutenant of Christ on earth; therefore, he possesses earthly jurisdiction as well. Bellarmine distinguished between possession of temporal jurisdiction, which of course Christ had, and *exercise* of that jurisdiction, which he maintained Christ steadfastly refused: "Mine is not the kingdom of this earth." Twentieth-century popes as well as theologians (such as John Courtney Murray) have adopted Bellarmine's reasoning to establish a scriptural line of demarcation between the realm of man and that of God. Bellarmine's position has not only been vindicated, but it has been adopted and institutionalized.

The boorish and frenzied response to Bellarmine's *Controversies*, even from learned Protestant divines, is inexcusable when you consider the scrupulousness and even charity of Bellarmine's reasoning. He did not fail to defend Protestants when he found them misrepresented in Catholic apologetics: "As for Calvin, his language is certainly faulty and so open to the interpretations put upon by Catholic writers. . . . But even though this be the case, after diligent and very careful examination of his text I am not at all willing to say that he believed or taught heresy in question, and I shall now briefly explain my reasons for putting a favorable construction on his words." Nevertheless Bellarmine's *Controversies* was greeted with shrill and hysterical tracts such as "Against Bellarmine and Kennel of Monks and Mendicants" and "Against Robert Bellarmine and the Universal Cohort of

Jebusites and Canaanites." Bellarmine was called, among other things, a harpy of Rome, a filthy harlot, the whore of Babylon, Romish vermin, a foul-mouthed hog, and an abominable hypocrite. Fellow Catholics fought back passionately, William Bishop terming one Bellarmine critic "by birth a mean tanner's son, who at his first coming to Oxford was glad to sweep and dress up chambers and play the drudge for a slender pittance." But Bellarmine stayed aloof from the name-calling and class-condescension.

He knew, as did the polemicists on both sides, that the ferocity of the response could be directly attributed to the success of *Controversies*. Not only did they convert many Protestants and woo back defecting Catholics, but they also made inroads in very high places: for example, Cardinal du Perron, who converted from Calvinism and went on to become one of the most distinguished Catholic apologists in France, told Bellarmine, "No book published in defence of the Church during the past thousand years equals, in my judgement, your *Controversies*." Equipped with the Bible and *Controversies*, Francis de Sales went into the wild, mountainous Huguenot country of Savoy, braving death and converting thousands of the most hostile Protestants to the Roman Catholic faith. In 1579 a contingent of British exiles embraced Catholicism and vowed to return to their country to labor for its conversion; a number of them ended up martyrs. Dr. John Reynolds of Oxford delivered no less than two hundred fifty lectures against Bellarmine but still could not stop the erosion of the Protestant base at his university.

Despite Bellarmine's enormous fame, he remained, in life, simple and unassuming. Visitors were struck by the way he went about his normal life; one Belgian priest observed in 1580, "When I was engaged with him in the service of the kitchen, and in washing and drying dishes, he did all this lowly work as energetically, carefully and exactly as if it were the big business of theology that occupied him, and never a word did he speak nor once did he look around." Bellarmine took very seriously his Jesuit vows of obedience and poverty: even when he was (against his will) made cardinal in 1599, he refused the usual entourage of servants and horses, and gave away most of his annual revenues. To relatives who importuned him for gifts, he cited passages from the Council of Trent noting that family members were to be helped only if they were poor, and in a manner no different from strangers in the same condition. No wonder that Bellarmine was trusted by a string of successive popes and Church authorities, and named to virtually every office and commission of his time.

Toward the end of his life Bellarmine was drawn into the controversy between the Jesuits and Dominicans over the issue of justification by grace — a question he had earlier encountered in his escapades with the Protestants. Bellarmine outlined the four possible positions and soberly analyzed each. He considered the writing of his fellow Jesuit Luis Molina, who held that divine grace owes its saving efficacy to consent of the will — this view, Molina and numerous others believed was the only way to vindicate both divine grace and free will. But Bellarmine noted that the reasoning implied that man's cooperation was necessary in order for God's grace to become redemptive; this suggests that God does not save unilaterally, but rather is dependent on man for this; Bellarmine concludes that such a diminution of power is "false and therefore rightly reprehended." But he is gentler on another Jesuit line — that grace does not depend on the consent of will but instead, the free consent of will is itself intrinsically determined by grace; this view, which appears to be the one held by Aquinas, Bellarmine had reservations about but would not condemn. In the entire matter, he concluded, "it is not possible easily to convict either party of manifest error since both admit the authority of the Councils of Orange and Trent, and each alleges on his own behalf at least apparent testimonies from Saint Augustine and Saint Thomas." Bellarmine proposed that the pope not try to arbitrate or resolve the Jesuit-Dominican contest but merely insist that it be prosecuted in an atmosphere of mutual charity and goodwill. The pope did not adopt Bellarmine's advice, so subsequent councils continued to fight it out; ultimately a new pope ascended the throne of Saint Peter and he put the whole matter to rest. It has not been taken up by another pope to this day, so that Bellarmine's detente appears once again to have prevailed.

Bellarmine died an old man in the year 1621, not even a year after he published his last book, ironically titled *The Art of Dying Well*. It took more than two centuries for him to be canonized because successive hordes of Franciscans, Jansenists, and Gallicans continued to oppose his positions on divine grace and the temporal authority of the pope. But the procrastinators eventually failed, and on May 13, 1923, Pope Pius XI beatified him. He was canonized in 1930 and declared a Doctor of the Church in 1931. His memory and ideas live on today, inspiring Catholics who understand that ecumenism does not mean giving up the central deposit of faith, and that Catholicism constantly needs pious and learned defenders to speak up with courage against ever-present sophists and malcontents seeking to undermine the one holy Catholic and apostolic Church.

thérèse of lisieux's

story of a soul

NEARLY one hundred years ago — on September 8, 1890 to be exact — some very unusual wedding invitations were prepared by a young woman who would have a great impact on the Church. The invitations said:

Almighty God
Creator of Heaven and Earth
Supreme Sovereign of the Universe
and
The Most Glorious Virgin Mary
Queen of the Court of Heaven
Invite you to the Spiritual Marriage of their august Son
Jesus
King of Kings and Lord of Lords
with
Little Therese Martin

With a touch of sardonic wit the notice concluded, "It was not possible to invite you to the wedding feast held on the Mountain of Carmel, September 8, 1890, as only the heavenly court was admitted, but you are nevertheless invited to the At Home [celebration] tomorrow, the day of eternity when Jesus, the Son of God, will come on the clouds of heaven to judge the living and the dead in the full splendor of His majesty. The hour being uncertain, you are asked to hold yourself in readiness to watch."

This lovely little notice was written by a frail young woman whom Pope Pius X called "the greatest saint of modern times," Thérèse of Lisieux. Her story is truly one of the most startling in Church history. Born in 1873, she was little-known during her life, lived a brief and rather uneventful twenty-four years, and died in an obscure convent with only a handful of nuns at her side. Within a few decades, she has developed a worldwide following, helped bring about countless conversions, and generated interest surpassing numerous other saints with much more spectacular achievements to their credit. *The Story of a Soul*, Thérèse's spiritual autobiography, has been repeatedly cited as the instrument of her powerful appeal.

The amazing fact about Thérèse's life is that it resonates with the same total commitment to Christ that we find in Thomas à Kempis or Teresa of Ávila — but here is a young woman saying these things in the modern era, in cosmopolitan France at the turn of the century, a short distance from the Eiffel Tower, an institute dedicated to Darwin, an Impressionist museum, a popular health spa. Thérèse stands in firm and vibrant challenge to these symbols of modernity. Yet there is no trace of archaism or obsolescence about her prose or her personality; they leap out at you, passionate, imploring, insistent, alive in body and soul.

"I was seized with such a violent love for God that I can't explain it except by saying it felt as though I were totally plunged into fire. Oh! What fire and what sweetness at one and the same time. I was on fire with love, and I felt that one minute more, one second more, and I would not be able to sustain this ardor without dying. I understood then what the saints were saying about these states which they experienced so often. As for me, I experienced it only once and for one single instant."

Thérèse's *Story of a Soul* is a great work because of its contrite passion, its fierce and yet humble obeisance before the Almighty, its frightful and yet daring account of a young woman who hurled herself into the furnace of God's love. In this book we get a glimpse of that fidelity, that true love, of which earthly attachments are only a poor approximation. With rapt attention, perhaps even a trace of envy, we read a simple girl's romance with Jesus Christ whom she adored as her Savior. Is it possible, we wonder, that God could be an equally vital spirit animating our lives? If it could happen to little Thérèse, an average girl distinguished only by the fervency of her quest, millions of people now understand that this experience can be theirs as well.

Thérèse was born on January 2, 1873, in Alençon, France, to prosperous and devout Catholic parents. She was the youngest of five daughters, although other siblings were conceived and died in childbirth or in sickness. She was a high-strung little girl who enjoyed donkey rides and holidays on the seashore. A pet lover, she kept rabbits, goldfish, silkworms, and a spaniel named Tom. That she was moody is evident from something her mother once said: "She flings herself into the most dreadful rages when things don't go as she wants them. She rolls on the ground as if she's given up hope of anything ever being right again. Sometimes she's so overcome that she chokes."

Fortunately this intensity was, early on, channeled into piety, a fact for which Thérèse gives full credit to her parents. She tells the story of the time her younger sister came to her with a basket of clothes, ribbons, and other goodies: "Choose what you want," she said, and Thérèse replied with a laugh, "I choose everything." Later Thérèse realized that her aspiration, "to be a saint," entailed equal dedication. "My God, I choose all. I do not want to be a saint by halves. I am not afraid to suffer for you. I fear only one thing — that I should keep my own will. So take it, for I choose all that You will." Thérèse's autobiography frequently alternates between anecdotes of infancy and mature spiritual outpourings like this. From childhood, when she feels "the attraction of goodness," it seems a dizzyingly fast transition to deep sanctity:

"One Sunday when I was looking at a picture of Our Lord on the Cross, I saw the Blood coming from one of his hands, and I felt terribly sad to think that it was falling to the earth and that no one was rushing forward to catch It. I determined to stay continually at the foot of the Cross and receive It. I knew that I should then have to spread It among other souls. The cry of Jesus on the Cross — 'I am thirsty' — rang continually in my heart and set me burning with a new, intense longing. I wanted to quench the thirst of my Well-Beloved and I myself was consumed for a thirst for souls. I was concerned not with the souls of priests but with those of the great sinners which I wanted to snatch from the flames of hell."

Throughout her autobiography Thérèse refers to herself as "God's little flower," an image she sustains with clarity and variety throughout. For instance, she raises the question of how people on earth seem to enjoy such unequal shares of divine blessing — with even great sinners such as Saint Augustine granted reprieve, while upright pagans go through life only dimly hearing about Jesus Christ — and answers it with a metaphor.

In nature, she says, "The splendor of the rose and the whiteness of the lily do not rob the little violet of its scent nor the daisy of its simple charm. . . . If every flower wanted to be a rose, spring would lose its loveliness and there would be no wild flowers to make the meadows gay." So also, in God's "book of nature," God creates both saints and lesser saints, and people of varying capacities and dispositions. Each has a special individual plan and "perfection consists in doing His will, in being that which He wants us to be."

A bit later, with a characteristic switch of analogies, Thérèse explains why heaven's mansions are differently furnished. "God does not give equal glory in heaven to all His chosen," she says. If you fill a big tumbler and a little thimble with water, and wonder which is fuller, you realize that they are both full to the brim, and it is impossible to put more water in either. So too "in heaven God will give His chosen their fitting glory and the last will have no reason to envy the first."

As a child Thérèse's deeply religious disposition resulted in memorable dreams. She tells of the time she saw two horrible little devils perched on a barrel. "They were astonishingly lively in spite of the heavy chains on their feet." Suddenly, seeing her, they leapt down from the barrel and began to clank around the living room. "These wretched little imps were running about the tables and didn't know what to do to escape from my gaze." They cantered about, "as if crazy with despair." Thérèse concludes, "I think God has let me remember this to prove to me that a soul in a state of grace need fear nothing from devils, for they are so cowardly that they flee from the gaze of a child."

Thérèse's mother died of breast cancer in 1877, when Thérèse was only four, and her fertile imagination, until then so alive and happy, lapsed into despondency and lethargy. "I was only happy if no one took any notice of me, and I couldn't endure being with strangers." Relatives and friends attest to Thérèse's almost neurotic isolation.

"God's little flower would never have survived if He had not poured His warmth on her. She was still too frail to stand up to rain and storm. But Jesus gave her . . . the soft airs of spring, even amidst the bleak winter of her suffering." Thérèse vividly describes her first confession; despite her general sorrowful condition, "I left the confessional happier and more lighthearted than I had been before." Feast days were also intervals in her suffering: "I loved it when the Blessed Sacrament was carried in procession, for it gave me such joy to scatter flowers beneath the feet of God."

In 1881 Thérèse enrolled at the Benedictine Abbey at Lisieux. Her older sister Pauline, who was her "second mother" since her real parent died, left the next year to join the Carmelite cloister, shortly to be followed by another sister, Marie. Thérèse's anguish deepened; in late 1882 she suffered recurrent headaches. Nothing appeared to do any good, until one day Thérèse and her sisters knelt before the statue of the Virgin Mary and prayed. "Suddenly the Blessed Virgin glowed with a beauty beyond anything I had ever seen. Her face was alive with kindness and infinite tenderness, but it was her enchanting smile which really moved me to the depths. My pain vanished and two great tears crept down my cheeks — tears of pure joy. . . . The little flower had come back to life." Slowly Thérèse regained strength.

At a tender age, even before her teens, Thérèse aspired to be a saint. She loved Joan of Arc and she read tales of Arthurian chivalry in her youth, but somehow "I was made to understand that the glory I was to win would never be seen during my lifetime." Indeed she would not perform great miracles or execute glorious deeds. Rather, she would simply open her heart and soul to God's interminable rush of love. With precocious audacity, Thérèse ventures, "My glory will consist in becoming a great saint."

Thérèse never really fell in love, as other great saints did — for example, Augustine of Hippo or Teresa of Ávila. She regards this not as deprivation but as good fortune. "I've seen so many souls, dazzled by this deluding light, fly into it and burn their wings like silly moths. . . . I know that Jesus considered me too weak to be exposed to temptation. If I had seen this false light shining before me, I should have been wholly destroyed. . . . I should have fallen as low as Magdalene. I've been saved from that only by the great mercy of God."

At this point the reader of Thérèse should be careful. It is tempting to consider this tone of girlish helplessness to be the plaintive whine of a girl who never experienced life's keener pleasures, indeed never dared to pursue them, finding in religion an evasion and a crutch. But despite Thérèse's religious self-abasement (which comes from a recognition at a very early age of her own dependence on Christ's redemptive grace), Thérèse is a young woman of unusual courage and boldness, fully human in her depth of feeling, discovering in Christ and in Catholicism not an escape from life but an affirmation of it, not a truncation of experience but an extension of it through eternity, not a diminution of feeling but a consummation of love.

Her evocation of prayer to her dead siblings, for instance, is worthy of sublime comparison to Dante's great account of the lovers Paolo and Francesca. "I spoke to the four little angels who had gone to heaven ahead of me," Thérèse writes, "for I thought that they had never known either grief or fear, they would be sure to have pity on their poor little sister suffering on earth. With childlike simplicity I told them that, as I was the youngest of the family, I had always been most tenderly loved by my sisters and that if they themselves had remained on earth they would have given me similar love. That they were in heaven seemed no reason why they should forget me. On the contrary, they should draw on the divine treasury and obtain peace for me and thus show me that in heaven one still knew how to love. I hadn't to wait long for an answer. Waves of delicious peace soon flooded my soul and I knew that I was loved in heaven as well as earth."

On December 25, 1886, Thérèse experienced what she calls her "complete conversion." She returned from Christmas Mass to open her presents, all tucked in her shoes, in the fireplace. Unexpectedly, her father expressed irritation at the childishness of this annual event. "Thank goodness it's the last time we shall have this kind of thing." Thérèse rushed to her room, shocked and tearful, but then she felt a deep awareness of spiritual growth. "Jesus wanted to free me from the faults of childhood, so He took away its innocent pleasures." Thérèse wiped away her tears and ran downstairs to open her presents. But her youthful pique had vanished; indeed she was a different woman. From then on, she says, a new phase in her life began. She was only thirteen, but she had reached spiritual adulthood.

The next year Thérèse made her fateful decision, and told her father that she wanted to follow her sisters into the Carmelite cloister. She was fourteen years old, and yet, "if scholars who had spent their lives in study had questioned me, I am sure they'd have been amazed to come across a child who understood the secrets of perfection, secrets which all their learning couldn't reveal to them, for one has to be poor in spirit to understand them." Thérèse was uncontrollably keen: "The divine call was so urgent that, if necessary, I'd have plunged through flames to follow Jesus."

But others took a more cautious view. Her uncle, for example, said she should wait until she was seventeen; her enthusiasm was "against all human prudence" and her premature enrollment "would do great harm to religion." Local officials at Carmel offered to consider the matter, but they were, to put it mildly, dubious. Thérèse had a meeting with the bishop, who asked if she had wanted to enter Carmel for a long time.

"Oh, yes, for a very long time."

"Come, come," he said. "It can hardly have been for fifteen years."

"That's true, but it's not much less, for I've longed to give myself to God ever since I was three."

It is easy to see how Thérèse's assurances, given in all seriousness, could arouse mirth and perhaps even derision in elders. Bureaucratic delays, however, caused Thérèse tremendous gloom. "God afflicted me with a most grievous martyrdom. . . . It brought sharply home to me the bitter grief felt by the Blessed Virgin and Saint Joseph as they searched for the Child Jesus." Thérèse felt totally lost and abandoned, an experience she likens in her autobiography to Saint John's "dark night of the soul."

In November that year Thérèse and her father made a pilgrimage to Rome, which included an audience with Pope Leo XIII. There the pontiff stood, resplendent in purple, surrounded by cardinals and other dignitaries. A priest accompanying Thérèse warned that it was "absolutely forbidden" to speak to the Holy Father, but when her turn came, she could not resist. "Most Holy Father," she said, "to mark your jubilee, allow me to enter Carmel at fifteen." Immediately the vicar general intervened, informing the pope that Thérèse was "only a child" and the matter was being considered by the authorities. "Very well, my child," Pope Leo said. "Do whatever they say." Thérèse intrepidly tried again: "O most Holy Father, if you say yes, everybody will be only too willing." But the pope was firm. "You will enter if God wills," he said; then he blessed her. Thérèse was disappointed, she confesses, yet she felt peace that comes from submission to God's will. Only a month later the bishop approved her application, her uncle's resistance melted, and on April 9, 1888, she was received into Carmel of Lisieux, where she would spend the rest of her short life.

"My longing was at last fulfilled," Thérèse reports. "There was nothing transitory about my happiness. It wasn't an illusion which disappeared after my first few weeks in the convent. . . . I found that a nun's life was just what I imagined it would be."

It was certainly not uninterrupted bliss, dancing around the Maypole, and eating sweet vegetables from the ground. Thérèse endured the severe trials imposed by the prioress, Sister Marie de Gonzague. "God permitted that she was *very severe*, without even being aware of it," Thérèse writes. "I was unable to meet her without having to kiss the floor." Only one with Thérèse's determination and holiness could add, "I know that she loved me very much," indeed could later write her a letter thanking her "for not sparing me." Sister Gonzague's purgatory, Thérèse concludes, was "firm in valuable training, a priceless favor, for what should I have become if I had been the pet of the community — as some people outside the convent thought I was?" These are Thérèse's thoughts about a woman who would berate her publicly for overlooking a cobweb while cleaning the cloister.

It was when one of Thérèse's cousins, Jeane Guerin, married a local doctor that Thérèse began to meditate on the notion of Christ as her heavenly spouse. "She told me of all the care she lavished on her husband . . . and I said to myself: it's not going to be that a woman will do more for her husband, a mere mortal, than I will do for my beloved Jesus." She sought an intimate but direct relationship with Christ, a holiness that relished not miracles or mind-boggling feats but routine rapport with the Almighty. "That kind of sanctity strikes me as the truest, the holiest," Thérèse tells us. "It's the sort I want, for it is free of all illusions."

Thérèse loved her gardening tasks at Carmel. "Outside in the world young men give their sweethearts pretty nosegays of flowers. Jesus did not forget this. To adorn His altar I received masses of my favorite flowers — cornflowers, poppies, and marguerites." Even as she exults in these metaphors, though, Thérèse connects them with self-understanding. "From my earliest days I have believed that the Little Flower would be plucked in the springtime of her life."

The section of *The Story of a Soul* describing Thérèse's meditations in the convent is profuse with pristine joy and celestial peace. "Now I wish for only one thing," Thérèse writes, "to love Jesus even unto folly." She was never very bookish and indeed "if I glance at a book, no matter how good and moving, my heart at once

143

contracts and I read without understanding." But with Scripture, the Gospels "are always showing me new ways of looking at things. I am always finding hidden and mysterious meanings in them." Thérèse also learns from spiritual insights communicated directly by Christ through prayer. "Jesus, the doctor of souls, can teach without words. I have never heard him speak, but I know He is within me. He guides and inspires me every moment of the day."

Thérèse's aspiration to be a great saint remains with her, but she is somewhat intimidated by the reputations of the saints of old. "I look for some means of going to heaven by a little way which is very short and very straight," she says, "a little way that is quite new." Then, with a modern twist, "We live in an age of inventions. We need no longer climb laboriously up flights of stairs; in well-to-do houses there are lifts." Thérèse intends her simple openness to God's grace, unencumbered by any futile efforts of her own, to serve as a kind of spiritual elevator to take her up to heaven.

She is hesitant to outline her spiritual travails "lest I should blaspheme." Nevertheless, she tells a chilling story about the voice of unbelievers mocking her in the darkness while she prayed. "You dream of light," these voices tell her, "of a fragrant land; you dream that the Creator will be yours forever and you think you will one day leave behind this fog in which you languish. Hope on. And look forward to death. But it will give you, not what you hope for, but a still darker night, the night of annihilation." Terrible as these assaults on the soul were, Thérèse gives thanks for them. "How gentle and merciful God is," she says. "He sends me this heavy cross just at the time when I am strong enough to bear it."

In a wonderful discussion of the virtue of charity Thérèse writes, "I realize that true charity consists in putting up with all one's neighbor's faults, never being surprised by his weakness, and being inspired by the least of his virtues." She adopts this attitude with fellow nuns. "When the devil tries to show me the faults of a sister, I hasten to think of all her virtues and how good her intentions are. I tell myself that though I have seen her commit sin, she may very well have won many spiritual victories of which I know nothing because of her humility. What seems a fault to me may very well be an act of virtue because of the intention behind it."

During meditation at Carmel a nun frequently bothered Thérèse with her constant fidgeting. "I could not tell you how it irritated me," Thérèse writes. "What I wanted to do was turn and stare at her until she stopped her noise." But Thérèse decided instead to patiently endure it, partly not to upset the sister, partly for the love of God. "So I made no fuss, even though sometimes I was soaked with sweat under the strain and my prayer was nothing but the prayer of suffering." Remember, Thérèse always was very impressionable even as a little girl. She simply could not take her mind off the transgressing sister. "At last I tried to find some way of enduring this suffering calmly and even joyfully. So I did my best to enjoy this unpleasant little noise. Instead of trying not to hear it, which was impossible, I strove to listen to it as if it were a first class concert. My meditation was spent in offering this concert to Jesus." This is the voice of a woman who has found extraordinary control of her emotions, through exertion of will and through grace. Through such habitual exertions is virtue sharpened and expanded so it becomes indistinguishable from the rest of our sinful selves.

She is just as self-effacing about the virtue of humility. "If an artist's canvas could think and speak," she writes, "it would know that it owes all its beauty not to the brush but to the artists who guide the strokes. And the brush cannot take any of the credit for the masterpiece it paints for it knows that artists often use the feeblest and most faulty tools." Thérèse tells her Mother Superior that "I am a tiny brush that Jesus has chosen to paint His likeness in the souls who have been entrusted to me. . . . To me, Mother, you are the big valuable brush held lovingly in the hand of Jesus when he wishes to accomplish some great work. I am the very tiny brush he uses afterwards for the unimportant details."

Obedience is stressed by Thérèse virtually without caveat. "How happy nuns are. The will of their superiors is their only compass and so they are always certain of travelling in the right direction. They can never fall mistaken, even if they are certain their superiors are wrong. If, though, one stops being guided by this compass for a single moment, the soul strays into a desert where the waters of grace quickly fail." Notable about Thérèse, and all great spiritualists, is how the vector of their mysticism never moves outside the parameters of orthodoxy, and moreover how unfailingly dedicated they are to the pope and the Church. Far lesser lights of our own day, claiming the mantle of spiritual charisma, insist on leaping outside the circle of magisterial authority; they would do well to heed the example of their forbears.

Thérèse understands something that all readers will find implicit in her autobiography — godliness does not diminish humanity. "To offer oneself to God does not mean that one loses anything at all of one's natural tenderness," she writes. "It is just the opposite, for this tenderness deepened as it becomes purified by centering on divine things." Thus Thérèse finds that her relationship with other sisters takes on a depth and closeness that is rarely found in the secular world; it is divine love which gives them both their special aroma.

Finally Thérèse gives us her thoughts on prayer. "I cannot bring myself to hunt through books for beautiful prayers. There are so many of them that I get a headache. Besides, each prayer seems lovelier than the next. . . . I tell God very simply what I want and He always understands. For me, prayer is an upward leap of the heart, an untroubled glance toward heaven, a cry of gratitude and love which I utter from the depths of sorrow as well as from the heights of joy."

Aware of the great travels of saints such as Francis of Assisi and Francis Xavier, Thérèse boldly utters a forbidden desire: "If only I were a priest!" She would, she speculates, lovingly share Christ with the faithful. "Like the prophets or doctors of the Church, I would enlighten souls. I should like to wander throughout the world . . . not satisfied unless I preach the Gospel in every quarter of the globe and even in the most remotest islands. Nor should I be content to be a missionary for only a few years; I should like to be one from the creation of the world to the end of time." Thérèse also longs to be a martyr. "But I don't want to suffer just one torment. I should like to have suffered them all to be satisfied. Like you, my adorable Jesus, I want to be scourged and crucified. I want to be flayed like Saint Bartholomew. Like Saint John I want to be flung into boiling oil. Like Saint Ignatius of Antioch I long to be ground by the teeth of wild beasts. . . . With Saint Agnes and Cecilia, I want to offer my neck to the sword of the executioner and, like Saint Joan of Arc, murmur the name of Jesus at the stake." But Thérèse isn't leading a petition drive for women's ordination here, or engaging in nostalgia for the time of the Roman persecutions. Quickly she checks these musings: "Now what can you say to all my silliness? Is there anywhere in the world a tinier, weaker soul than mine?"

The Story of a Soul ends where it began, in an invocation of undying love for Christ. "At last I have found my vocation. My vocation is love! I have found my place in the bosom of the Church." It is this love that redeems Thérèse, and it is this love that elevates her autobiography from a rather mundane tract into a spiritual classic. "I sit, as it were, and cast my fishing line at random into the little stream flowing through my heart," Thérèse humbly tells her Mother Superior. "Then I offer you my tiny fish just as they were caught." But these little fish are souls, and Thérèse is on no ordinary expedition — she is recounting the story of a great catch (herself) at the hands of the Fisher of Men, Christ himself. Thus *The Story of a Soul* is the one tall tale, the one fishing story, that is utterly believable, and inspiring as well.

Thérèse didn't compose it voluntarily; she was asked to write her childhood memories by her sisters Marie and Pauline, who were her seniors at Carmel; she took their advice as an instruction. Later, Thérèse's Mother Superior asked her to update and complete her early account, and the two volumes — written in longhand under the nocturnal flame of an oil lamp — were later edited, divided into chapters, and published jointly as *The Story of a Soul*. Thérèse finished her masterpiece just before she died, penning the last sentence under the chestnut trees in the garden of Carmel, as nuns stopped by one by one to say good-bye to the "little flower."

"What I have written will do a lot of good," Thérèse said. "It will make the kindness of God better known." A month later she died of tuberculosis: the painful coughing finally stopped, and she was buried in the chapel at Carmel. "After my death," she told her sister Pauline, "I don't want to be surrounded by wreaths and flowers." This baffling statement should be understood as Thérèse's transition from metaphor to reality. The "little flower" was no more, literally as well as figuratively. Her soul had entered into eternal union with its Maker, and being plucked from its mortal state, it could no longer be compared, in limited human terms, to a daisy or a cornflower. After death, we no longer stand in need of flowery language. The Garden of Eden awaits the blessed in a most literal way.

Thérèse died at the age of twenty-four, but very few seemed to notice. French life swilled and chattered and waltzed on, in the galleries and cafés and villas. The convent at Carmel, too, went about its usual business, in its spartan way, surrounded by pillars and seats of stone and wood. But a year after Thérèse's death, *The Story of a Soul* was published in an edition of two thousand copies. A local Carmelite nun declared it inadequate. "Age and experience would have changed her opinions," she observed. Sales of the book gathered steady momentum, however, reaching into the tens of thousands and soon millions. Today the book has been translated into thirty-eight languages and is one of the best-sellers of the twentieth century.

Literary critics and scholars know that *The Story of a Soul* is no literary or stylistic triumph. Shakespeare would not have been impressed, and James Joyce would probably snicker at the lack of originality. Nevertheless Thérèse would not have minded them; she was never attracted to outstanding genius; hers was the contented province of simple truth, accessible to all, because it was for all men that Christ died. Thérèse's autobiography has universal appeal and is enjoyed and taken to heart by businessmen, farmers, and grandmothers alike. A book so universal in its appeal can be forgiven its hackneyed phrases, because there is not one hackneyed thought or experience in here. Thérèse makes old feelings and ideas seem "ever ancient, ever new," in Augustine's phrase.

A mere twenty-eight years after her death, on May 17, 1925, Thérèse of Lisieux was canonized by Pope Pius XI, and thus she realized her dream of becoming a "great saint." Shortly thereafter she was declared patron saint of the missions, with Francis Xavier. Later she was named secondary patron of France with Saint Joan of Arc. Exalted company indeed.

Yet Thérèse would most have delighted not in attainment of human grandeur and accolade but in the recovery of spiritual simplicity and innocence — "the little way of spiritual childhood" she calls it in her autobiography. We are all called by Christ to follow this path, dramatized by the Catholic saint who found her way to heaven through love.

jacques maritain's

integral humanism

MUCH of the moral argument of our day focuses on the issue of "secular humanism." On one side are the fundamentalists who identify in secular humanism a mortal enemy seeking to annihilate every vestige of religion from public life, to reduce moral truth to arbitrary private preference, and to permit if not subsidize social evils such as pornography, drugs, and abortion in the name of "individual choice." On the other side are political and theological liberals who usually express bafflement at the very concept of secular humanism, as if it were a noise, not a word. Even if such a term had meaning, they insist, it stands for nothing more than tolerance, compassion, and individual rights. The fundamentalists, they allege, are religious fanatics who seek to extirpate, in the name of God, basic freedoms of religion and expression that we have come to enjoy.

Missing from this unfortunate dispute is that "third voice" which cherishes both divine truth and human freedom, which allows no incompatibility between pursuing God and living a fully human life, which embraces those aspects of modernity that encourage a freer, fuller dedication to the call of the transcendent. Jacques Maritain's

Integral Humanism offers an alternative to the somewhat narrow stridency of fundamentalism and the undiscriminating permissiveness of secularism. The distinguished French philosopher teaches us how we can be liberal of mind and democratic in our politics while at the same time being fully Christian. His writing is a vindication of the possibility of the Gospel command to be "in the world but not of it." Maritain is both distinctively Catholic yet genuinely ecumenical; he is both otherworldly and wholly down-to-earth; he believes that citizens of the modern age have distinctive secular and religious responsibilities, not identical but compatible, and these entail dealing separately with the realms of Caesar and God. Perhaps the preeminent Thomas Aquinas scholar of the twentieth century, Maritain applied Thomistic concepts and categories to illuminate contemporary problems, thus giving Catholic modern thought new luminescence and relevance.

Jacques Maritain was born in Paris on November 18, 1882. His father was a nonpracticing Catholic, his mother a Protestant; their family embodied the loose and incoherent ecumenism of *fin de siecle* France. At the University of Paris, at the age of nineteen, Maritain met the young woman who would change his life, a Russian-born Jew named Raïssa. They would find in each other partners for life, more importantly partners in a quest for truth leading up and down the windy stairs of skepticism right into the portal of the Catholic Church. Raïssa Oumanisoff became Mrs. Jacques Maritain on November 26, 1904.

Although both Maritain and his wife exulted in the scientific discoveries that captivated the world of the early twentieth century, they found in them no answers to the questions that men have always asked about themselves and their universe: Why does it exist? Why are we here? What is our destiny? How do we get there? Why is there so much suffering in the world? Why is there joy? The writings of the tortured but deeply spiritual Léon Bloy and Charles Péguy drew the Maritains into a study of Christian history and mysticism, then into the unfailing depths of Scripture, finally to a gradual but sure conviction of the truth of Catholicism. They were baptized on June 11, 1906.

It was shortly after that, in Germany at the Sorbonne, that Raïssa Maritain discovered the *Summa* of Aquinas; for the second time, she writes, she "fell in love." Jacques on reading Thomas discovered that he was "already a Thomist without even knowing it," so deeply were Thomas's ideas embedded in the fabric of human intelligence and human experience. In 1913 Maritain's lectures on "The Philosophy of Bergson and Christian Philosophy," which amounted to a Thomistic critique of Henri Bergson (favored thinker of the European cognoscenti), launched the young French thinker to international fame. An unexpected financial legacy from a young soldier named Pierre Villard, killed in World War I, whom Maritain had met and corresponded with, allowed Maritain to open a center for Thomistic study and to hold seminars and accommodate discussion groups — the first gust of the Thomistic revival that would sweep the Continent and leave an indelible mark on modern Catholicism.

Those were troubling and confusing times in Europe. The Russian revolution unleashed the specter of Marxist Communism, which some Christians found a consummation of Gospel ideals, others a godless menace to be resisted unto death. Among the latter group were the intellectuals of the *Action Française*, who united around the brilliant Charles Maurras to revive the virtue of the *ancien régime.* Although initially sympathetic to them because of their moral and intellectual seriousness, Maritain later regretted his association because of complicity by these traditionalists in the rise of Fascism in Europe. Yet, early on, Maritain diagnosed the equally homicidal tendency of Communism — the political challenge of his life was to find a humanizing alternative to these dangerous swirling currents of left-wing and right-wing fanaticism. Rejecting what he called "the despotic notion" by which "the state exists in its own right . . . superimposed on the body politic or dominating entirely . . . enjoying supreme power," Maritain offered a vision of democratic governance in which state power would be limited and entirely oriented toward the common good of the citizens. "Man is by no means for the state. The state is for man," Maritain writes in one of his classic political tracts, *Man and State.*

It was not just the power and clarity of his thought but also the evident goodness and simplicity of Maritain's character that drew others to him. His life intersected with some of the greatest politicians, statesmen, moralists, and literary figures of his day, and all were deeply affected by him. Thomas Merton, author of *The Seven Storey Mountain,* writes: "I was introduced to Maritain at the Catholic Book Club, where this most saintly philosopher gave a talk on Catholic Action. I only spoke a few conventional words to Maritain, but the impression you got from this gentle, stooping Frenchman with much gray hair was one of tremendous kindliness and simplicity and godliness. That was enough; you did not need to talk to him. I came away feeling very comforted that there was such a person in the world."

Integral Humanism, Maritain's masterpiece, was written in 1936 against the backdrop of bedlam and angst all over Europe. Depression in America, extended to other continents as well, directed many eyes toward Communism as the new social organization of the future. European decadence caused many to look to the rhythmic and confident goose-step of Fascism as an equally invigorating solution. The middle-of-the-road answer was the paternalistic state whose tentacles reached farther and deeper into the private lives of citizens. In the realm of theology, neo-modernism was the fashion, seeking to bring Christianity into harmony with the new age, but at the same time questioning if not abandoning many of the traditional teachings of the faith. *Integral Humanism* dissects each of these approaches, often with considerable empathy and goodwill, ultimately rejecting them for a unified *weltanshauung*, or world-view, that achieves their goals in a better, richer way.

Maritain begins his philosophy at the usual starting point — himself, a man, the source of philosophizing. Nobody is against humanity, he says, but "to propose to man only the human . . . is to betray man and to wish his misfortune, because by the principal part of him, which is the spirit, man is called to better than a purely human life." This is no Christian discovery, Maritain notes — the ancient Greeks, starting with Plato and Aristotle, italicized this point. Man's nature includes both a corporal and a spiritual or transcendent aspect. We should not, Maritain warns, define humanism in such a way as to exclude all reference to the supernatural which has, throughout history and in every culture, exercised an important influence on the mind and culture of human beings.

Maritain's integral humanism, his Christian humanism, builds on the heritage of Western civilization. The West was intellectually shaped by alloying the highest elements of reason from Greco-Roman thought with the highest reach of Christian revelation. All-enduring dilemmas, such as that between free will and grace, are ultimately generated by the tension between reason (which propels will) and revelation (the fount of grace). Despite the tension, Maritain believes that intercourse between pagan rationalism and Christian revelation has been enriching; correctly interpreted, it produces an integrated Christian perspective capable of harnessing the highest energies of both mind and soul, of leading man to the zenith of human wisdom as well as divine truth.

Errors are usually produced by suppressing one side or the other of this precarious balance, according to Maritain. Thus Protestants who advocate predestination believe that "there is no longer any free will; it has been killed by original sin. . . . This is the theology of grace without freedom." At the other end of the seesaw are the secularists, whose humanism rejects God either as an unnecessary crutch or an enemy of human autonomy. This, Maritain says, is the "metaphysic of freedom without grace." A truly integrated Christian humanism is a Catholic humanism that navigates between this Scylla and Charybdis. "As the pessimism of the Reformers overstressed the Christian datum of original sin, the optimism of the Renaissance overstressed . . . the conviction of the value of the human being." Some Renaissance thinkers believed man to be virtually a creature without limit, capable of knowledge without outside inspiration, joy without purification or asceticism. The Renaissance thinker "turns toward the documents of pagan antiquity with a fever which the pagans had not known." Socrates, who believed himself the wisest man in Athens because he understood his own limits and his own ignorance, would surely be embarrassed at the claims being made in his name, Maritain suggests.

He identifies two kinds of humanism: man-centered (or anthropocentric humanism) and God-centered (or theocentric humanism). "The radical vice of anthropocentric humanism has been its being anthropocentric, and not its being humanism," Maritain writes. The problem with an exclusive focus on man is that it is a recipe for man's dehumanization. Maritain wonders whether Darwinism, because of its implication that there is no discontinuity between man and lower beings, has undermined that structure of moral reasoning which has always distinguished man from the beasts. Has not Freud's emphasis on unconscious urges, dreams, and wish-fulfillment undercut human autonomy, human freedom, even human dignity? When individual man is reduced to atoms, propelled either by chemical transactions or inexplicable forces of instinct and desire, what becomes of the case for humanism? In what sense is a man to be considered special, unique, worthy of respect, and understanding? No wonder, Maritain suggests, that when humanism can no longer base its case on individual man, it turns to exaltation of collective man.

In his analysis of collectivism, Maritain notes that "among the original elements of Communism are also some Christian elements." Certainly the idea of the dignity of work, the sharing of rewards, the subordination of self-interest to the common good, are all conspicuously Christian themes. Communism, however, distorts and manipulates them to evil ends, according to Maritain. "Atheism is presupposed as the principle of the system — the starting point," he writes. "It is the spirit of the faith and sacrifice, 'the religious energies of the soul,' which Communism endeavors to drain off for its own uses."

Maritain scorns the idea of the proletariat as the agent of this-worldly redemption. "Not only are the proletariat's hands unstained by original sin or by the exploitation of man by man, but precisely because the proletariat is stripped of everything and occupies the lowest place in history, it is the bearer of human liberation." The Marxist implication, in other words, is that poverty and degradation by themselves confer virtue. Then the proletariat is authorized to unleash violence and hatred against the bourgeoisie, bringing about redemption through destruction. "Marx's humanism is pre-eminently a humanism of the Manichean type," Maritain says, referring to the early Christian heresy. "It asks that we reject into darkness . . . a whole part of the human heritage."

By contrast, the Christian view is that "at the new moment of the history of Christian culture, the creature will not be belittled or annihilated before God; and neither will it be rehabilitated without God or against God; it will be rehabilitated in God." Maritain calls for "humanism, but theocentric humanism, rooted where man has his roots, integral humanism, humanism of the Incarnation." In the Christian humanistic framework not only is bourgeois man transformed but all man is transformed in God — we "die unto ourselves" and Christ lives in us, as the Gospel promises.

Assessing the relationship of Christianity to human governance — the role of the state — Maritain eschews simpleminded statements such as "heaven belongs to God and earth belongs to Satan." He writes, "The true doctrine about the world and the temporal city is that they are the kingdom simultaneously of man, of God, and of the devil. The world is a closed field which belongs to God by right of creation; to the devil by right of conquest, because of sin; to Christ by right of victory over the conqueror, because of the passion." The Christian thus operates in a zone of ambiguity or ambivalence; his duty in the world "is to dispute with the devil his domain, to wrest it from him."

We should not confuse the world that is, with the world that is to come. "The world is saved, yes," Maritain writes, "it is delivered in hope; it is on the march toward the kingdom of God; but it is not holy, it is the Church which is holy." The world is only "a refraction of the world of the gospel." Temporal solutions only approximate eternal solutions, just as Thomas Aquinas wrote that the human law is only a faint copy of the divine law.

Maritain now proceeds to a grand view of the history of civilization. Of course the state should be concerned with the welfare of souls, he insists. Indeed, "In a sense an earthly city capable of the death sentence for the crime of heresy shows a greater care for the good of souls and a higher idea of the nobility of the human community, thus centered on truth, than a city which only knows how to mete out punishment for crimes against the body." Maritain knows, however, that "it was precisely here that human nature was inevitable to introduce its worst abuses . . . especially as the State ceased to act as an instrument of a legitimate spiritual authority superior to it, and arrogated to itself the right to act in all matters spiritual." Indeed Maritain locates state-sponsored violence of the Inquisition as the root of modern-day totalitarianism of the Marxist or Fascist variety.

In the modern world, Maritain argues, "A body politic can only be a Christian body politic within those walls unbeliever and believer live today and share in the same temporal common good." Believers should tolerate (although not necessarily approve) ways of worship removed from the true one, which is the Catholic one. This pluralistic approach, based on the foundation of equal rights, is theologically sound because it respects God's creatures as equal in his eyes; it also appreciates that free assent is essential to virtue. If good is coerced, it accrues no favor in God's eyes; God gave us a will so that we may voluntarily embrace his lordship over our lives.

For Maritain the earthly order has its own jurisdiction and justification, although it is ultimately subordinate to the transcendent order. It is possible, however, to agree on morality in this world while disagreeing about theological implications for the next world. For instance, a Catholic, a Protestant, and a Jew could dispute the existence and legacy of Christ while uniting in support of care of the sick, or in opposition to pornography and abortion. When Maritain was appointed French ambassador to the United Nations, he helped to formulate the landmark "Declaration on the Rights of Man" on precisely this premise.

"How," he asked, "is an agreement conceivable among men . . . who come from the four corners of the earth and who belong not only to different cultures and civilizations, but to different spiritual families and antagonistic schools of thought?" Maritain concluded, "Since the aim is a practical aim, agreement can be spontaneously achieved, not on common speculative notions, but on common practical notions, not on the affirmation of the same conception of the world, man and knowledge, but on the affirmation of the same set of convictions concerning action." The rights of man, in other words, represent the area of practical convergence between sharply differing ideologies and world-views.

Considering the specific aspects of a legitimate earthly order, Maritain stressed private ownership of property. "The remedy for the abuses of individualism must not be sought in the abolition of private property," Maritain warned. Rather, economic opportunity should be expanded so all citizens, or rather all families, have a chance to own property. Thus would men become stewards of creation as God intended. Thus would private property serve the common good.

Maritain foresaw later developments of science that would subordinate human emotion and well-being to the inevitability of technological advance. "Industry and technology should be placed at the service of man, yet despite themselves they have inevitably ended in making man the slave of industry and technology." Maritain accepts that machines and labor-saving devices and new inventions are good in themselves, but their ultimate value comes in being used in the right way. "We must choose between the idea of an industrial civilization and the idea of an essentially human one, for which industry is really only an instrument and is therefore subjected to laws that are not its own."

Maritain holds up the ideal of the Christian family as a formula for happiness and unity. He deplores feminist misunderstanding, which protests against the subjugation of women in the Church. "Christianity has given to woman — treated in the Orient especially, as an object of property — the sense of her dignity and personal liberty." The Christian family, for Maritain, is "founded on the union above all spiritual and sacramental to two persons engendering for an eternal destiny other living beings endowed with an imperishable soul." The fact that in most families it is men who provide and nourish the family, exercising their dominion in the world outside of work, and that women exercise primacy within the home, giving birth and taking care of children — these are ways to enhance the mutual dignity and love of couples, and not a violation of equality of rights.

As for political systems, Maritain is a resolute defender of democracy because it is based on human equality and human dignity. As democracy includes citizens in the process of shaping the future, it offers hope for a practical realization of the common good. Because it caters state activity to the welfare of the people, it tends to respect natural rights and human rights. The ideal democracy is one that is explicitly based on a religious premise — "In God We Trust." Maritain, who taught at Princeton University in the latter part of his life, wrote with particular affection of the American political system; he particularly appreciated the Declaration of Independence with its assertion that "All men are created equal and endowed by their Creator with certain unalienable rights, among these life, liberty and the pursuit of happiness."

Maritain understood that worldly politics is the art of the possible; he was thus allergic to Utopianism as well as its equal and opposite illusion — that because we cannot achieve Paradise, all this-worldly reform is fruitless and unnecessary. "The fear of soiling ourselves by entering the context of history is a Pharisaical fear," he writes in *Integral Humanism*. "We cannot touch the flesh of the human being without staining our fingers. To stain our fingers is not to stain our hearts. . . . Some seem to think that to put our hands into the real, to this concrete universe of human things and human relations where sin exists and circulates, is in itself to contract

162

sin, as if sin were contracted from without, not from within."

With Thomistic precision, Maritain's analysis of state power distinguishes between ends and means. We should make sure that we do not use illicit means to achieve worthwhile ends, he says. We should also ensure that the means correspond to the ends. In practical terms, this means that "the Christian must not refuse to use force, when it is absolutely necessary to repel evil." Pacifism for Maritain was the error of allowing wickedness to triumph because good refused to enter the fray for fear of contaminating itself. "All that is necessary for evil to triumph is for good men to do nothing," as Edmund Burke put it. On the other hand Maritain realized all too well that force is not the Christian way: "The Christian trembles at the necessity of having recourse to do it." It should always be a last resort.

In Church matters, Maritain stressed the distinction between the role of the priest and the role of the Catholic in the pew, a distinction that Pope John Paul II has taken up with vigor. Maritain's own life stands as a testament to a Catholic layman fulfilling to the utmost his lay calling in the Church. It is for laymen to apply the Catholic perspective to politics, to literature, and to scholarship, Maritain believed. The job of the clergy is not politics; theirs is the spiritual domain, which is infinitely grander and more important. Writing as an old man, Maritain would chastise clergy for aspiring to lay roles in the Church, and laymen for attempting to ascend to the pulpit. He always believed, as a good Thomist, that it is in fulfilling the function that is proper to us that we most truly achieve goodness and holiness.

"If the medieval Church directly formed and shaped the politics of Europe, it was because it had then the task

163

of making the temporal order emerge from chaos," Maritain writes. "Today the temporal organism exists, and is highly differentiated. It is not to the Church but to Christians as temporal members of this temporal organism that the transformation and regeneration according to the Christian spirit belongs. . . . It does not belong to the clergy to hold controls of properly temporal and political action."

Maritain's vision of an integrated and wholesome Christian life became the central theme of Vatican Council II. Maritain's influence was conspicuous in a number of the historic council's documents. Many of his themes — the importance of religious liberty, ecumenism rightly viewed, the dignity and the rights of the human person, fraternal feeling for the Jewish people, the role of the laity, and the recognition of the value of science, art, and democracy (which were all relatively new when he became their champion) — shone forth brightly at Vatican II. Maritain was correctly viewed as an exemplar of the liberal mind that had helped to "bring the Church into the modern world," the stated objective of the council.

It was surprising to many, therefore, when Maritain many years later published *The Peasant of Garonne.* "A shock to friend and foe alike. . . . It appears to call a halt to the modernist revolution that Maritain himself did much to inspire," the *New York Times* observed. Maritain was harshly critical of the excesses of neo-modernism that, according to him, had used the "spirit of Vatican II" to turn its plain language on its head. Maritain spurned the spiritual laissez-faire that permitted Catholics to believe whatever they wished, whether or not it conformed with doctrine, tradition, or the magisterium. Such an approach, Maritain predicted, was bringing about "the ruin of faith."

Ecumenism, for instance, Maritain viewed as being falsely and foolishly used as a vehicle for diluting Catholic doctrine, in some cases even for Christian surrender and abasement before other religions. "Let us beware of those brotherly dialogues in which everyone is in raptures while listening to the heresies, blasphemies, stuff and nonsense of the other," Maritain wrote. "If I truly love my neighbor, it will be painful for me to see him deprived of the truth that I happen to know." In other words ecumenism is an opportunity for evangelization, no less real for its being conducted in a spirit of love.

Throughout his life Maritain held up the objective of Thomas Aquinas — "to descend from revealed truth to the philosophies of our time in order to enlighten them, purify them." Just as Thomas Aquinas took what was noble and true in Aristotle and exalted it, and amended and transformed what was defective in order to make it true, so also Maritain strove to refashion the philosophies of his own time to bring them into synchrony with the enduring truth of Catholicism.

After a long life during which Maritain earned the reverence and affection of Catholic and non-Catholic alike, the great Thomist died of a heart attack on April 28, 1973. But from his works his voice still calls us to a true humanism that loves God while despising nothing that is in man: "Such humanism knows that the man is created from nothing and that everything which comes from nothing tends toward nothingness, and it also knows that man is the image of God and there is in man something more than man. It knows that a man dwells in a God who not only makes him love and move, but gives himself to a man and wants him to have for his object three divine persons themselves. It is humanism of redemptive incarnation, an evangelical humanism."

CLIVE Staples Lewis (better known as C.S. Lewis) was not a Roman Catholic, yet it is hard to imagine a more Catholic work in the twentieth century than *Mere Christianity*. Lewis himself appears to have thought so; in his own life he was propelled by the ideas of *Mere Christianity* closer toward the Catholic Church. He was an Anglo-Catholic when he died on November 22, 1963, but by several accounts he was on the verge of entering the Roman Church. Christopher Derrick, in his book *C.S. Lewis and the Church of Rome*, points out that Lewis believed in purgatory, in the necessity of good works, in opulence of the liturgy, in the Real Presence of Christ in the Eucharist, in apostolic succession, in the evil of artificial contraception. Was not Lewis then what Cardinal Newman was long suspected of being: a Catholic Anglican in camouflage?

Lewis's real importance is not his denomination, however. He was not a believer in Christian differentiation or schism. "Ever since I became a Christian I have thought that the best, perhaps the only, service I could do for my unbelieving neighbors was to explain and defend the belief that has been common to nearly all Christians at all times," Lewis writes in his introduction to *Mere Christianity*. He is content to be "merely Christian," to show how much is implied in that unassuming phrase. Denominational quarreling, Lewis knows, wins few converts from paganism and probably deters many. He also sensed what we now know — that in the second part of the twentieth century, the central issue is not Catholic versus Protestant, but rather belief in Christian truth versus unbelief. Because we find so many who deny fundamental Christian doctrines even within the Catholic and Protestant walls, the differences inside these denominations have grown wider than the distance that separates them. The pope today probably has more in common with born-again evangelical pastors than he does with some of the prominent dissenting Catholic theologians.

The virtue of *Mere Christianity* is that it draws the dividing line at the right point — between those who accept Christ and those who reject him. All else, as Shakespeare might say, is folly. Although he was not a professional theologian — perhaps because he was not — Lewis manages to make his point lucidly, gracefully, systematically, convincingly. It is no exaggeration to count him as the foremost popular apologist for the faith in our time. Very few names — G.K. Chesterton, Fulton Sheen — even offer competition. *Mere Christianity* is both original in its arguments and familiar in its analogies. Often the reader responds, "Why didn't I think of that?" Lewis is read with a combination of admiration and awe that metamorphoses into love. He is like Plutarch, Bunyan, or Dickens; you cannot help but be fond of the fellow. Persuasion is almost an accidental by-product of a reader's love affair with Lewis. Yet Lewis is best at buttressing and reinforcing the beliefs of lukewarm and wayward Christians. C.S. Lewis does not write for philosophical skeptics. He cannot persuade of God's existence people who refuse to admit their own existence.

Lewis was a professor of English literature at Oxford. Ever since his conversion to Christianity, he was something of an anomaly in the skeptical groves of academe. Many of his colleagues told him that they wished he would stick to analyses of *Hamlet* and *Beowulf*, staying clear of religious controversy. Not only was that considered pointless, but also terribly impolite, since it violated the etiquette of literary snobbishness.

The 1930s were a time of deep religious disillusionment — for a while there was hope for this-worldly Utopia, Paradise here on earth; but that was shattered as the clouds of totalitarianism assembled on the horizon. For those who would rather avoid the terrible questions arising about the nature of human brutality, and the possibility for human redemption, there was always the refuge of conventional, lowest-common-denominator Christianity, reduced to a few clichés about compassion and tolerance.

This is not what Lewis means by "mere Christianity" at all. His doctrine is "something not only positive but pungent, divided from all non-Christian beliefs by a chasm to which the worst divisions inside Christendom are not really comparable." He anticipates hostility even from "borderline Christians . . . men not exactly obedient to any communion." This Lewis finds "curiously consoling. It is at her center, where her truest children dwell, that each communion is really closest to every other spirit, if not in doctrine." *Mere Christianity* is the discovery, and the exposition, of this Christian epicenter, where Jesus sits.

Mere Christianity was delivered, as a series of radio talks, over British Broadcasting Corporation (BBC). Its colloquial style is a tremendous asset because it establishes a special rapport between the speaker (Lewis) and the reader. Lewis begins with conversation tidbits we hear every day: "How'd you like it if someone did the same to you?" "That's my seat, I was there first." "Leave him alone, he isn't doing you any harm." "Why should you shove in first?" "Come on, you promised." We pay little attention to these outbursts, Lewis writes; but what's curious about them is that "the man who makes them is not merely saying that the other man's behavior does not happen to please him. He is appealing to some kind of standard of behavior that he expects the other man to know about."

To this, the other man seldom replies, "To hell with your standard." Rather he tries to prove that what he is doing is not a violation of this standard of conduct, or if it is, there are special or extenuating circumstances. Lewis concludes, "It looks very much as if both parties had in mind some kind of Law or Rule of fair play or decent behavior or morality." This is what makes argument possible for human beings. Animals fight but men quarrel. To quarrel there must be something to quarrel about, some common ground that both combatants accept or take for granted. Lewis calls this the law of nature.

Although we hear much about Amazons who dominate their men and about cannibalism in primitive Africa, Lewis says that any impartial survey of civilizations — the ancient Greeks, Egyptians, Babylonians, Hindus, Chinese, Romans, modern Europeans — will demonstrate an impressive convergence of thinking on the norms by which people live. All men at all times have had a strong sense of right and wrong. Which people have ever cherished treason, or incest, or children beating their parents? Of course we will find an occasional exception, just as we will find natural states in which objects are weightless, or fall upward. With the moral law of human nature — as with nature's physical laws of nature and the law of human nature — the exception only proves the rule. The difference, however, is that nature's laws are inexorable, while man can choose to obey or disobey the law of human nature. This Lewis calls "free will."

It is no refutation of the law of human nature that people habitually break it, Lewis observes. People sometimes get their sums wrong, but this scarcely invalidates the addition or multiplication table. Lewis says that the foundation of all clear thinking about ourselves and the universe we live in is twofold: (1) there is a law of human nature, and (2) men break it.

Now Lewis pauses to answer a couple of obvious objections to his theory. Is not what he calls the law of human nature or "natural law" nothing more than herd instinct? Lewis concedes that, say, when a boy is drowning, we have a natural instinct to keep out of danger, an instinct for self-survival. At the same time we have an automatic impulse to help. Then, Lewis adds, "you will find inside you, in addition to these two impulses, a third thing which tells you that you ought to follow the impulse to help." This third force is not instinct but conscience. It is, in fact, that which arbitrates between conflicting impulses; it is a referee. Usually when instincts collide, Lewis says, the stronger of the two prevails, but with conscience it is most often the opposite — "it seems to tell us to side with the weaker of the two impulses."

Aristotle tells us that the right or virtuous thing to do must be understood in a given circumstance. Lewis, agreeing with this, points out that instincts are neither good nor evil in themselves. For instance, the fighting instinct is bad in most situations; but in a just war it is the moral duty of the soldier to encourage his fighting instinct. It is generous to feed a teaspoonful of sugar to a child, but not to a diabetic.

Nor is the natural law merely a function of social custom or convention — the argument of Rousseau and many modern philosophers. Lewis maintains that it is an error of reasoning to conclude from the fact that we learn something from our parents or teachers, that therefore it is a merely human convention or invention. We learn from our elders that the earth revolves around the sun; does this make that fundamental astronomical truth a mere fiction, sustained by idle custom? Of course social custom reinforces and buttresses the natural order of things, the natural law. That is the function of "civilization": to refine and systematize the law of human nature. But it is custom that takes its cues from natural law, not the other way around.

The oldest question in philosophy is why man should choose the moral course of action instead of the convenient or expedient one. Why, in other words, sacrifice self-interest for virtue? One common explanation is that in society men have a shared interest in playing by an unselfish set of rules. If everybody acted selfishly there would be chaos. We should act decently "because it is good for society," is this line of reasoning. But Lewis protests: "Why should I care what's good for society except when it happens to benefit me?" Why should I subordinate my interest to a collective interest? For me to care about the "good of society" is to presume I am unselfish in the first place; that can hardly be used to convince me to act unselfishly.

Lewis's point is that in our inner selves we all recognize the difference between convenience and morality. "A man occupying the corner seat in the train because he got there first, and a man who slipped into it while my back was turned and removed my bag, are both equally inconvenient. But I blame the second man and do not blame the first. I am not angry (except for a moment before I come to my senses) with a man who trips me up by accident; I am angry with a man who tries to trip me up even if he does not succeed." The law of human nature is distinctly impressed on our minds, and cannot be reduced to a function of instinct, convention, or convenience.

Now throughout human history there have been two broad ways of looking at the universe. The first, the materialist approach, assumes that man and his surroundings just happen to exist, perhaps they have always existed, and the chemicals of which they are comprised interact to produce their varieties of behavior; nothing lies outside the material system, whatever is thought to lie outside it is illusion. The problem with this approach, Lewis argues, is that while we cannot refute it in the case of the planets or the tides, we know it to be false in our own specific case — the case of human beings. The data being refuted in our own situation, where we are in a position to know, we are led to suspect its veracity in the case of the rest of the universe. In other words, an objective view of ourselves leads us to prefer the alternative hypothesis about the universe — it is not senselessly material, but rather, its material objects operate according to some sort of plan or order that exists apart from, and superior to, the universe itself. We are led to suspect a creator, a governing being, a God.

Does this view strike fashionable intellectuals of today as not progressive, as "turning back the clock" to those dark days of medieval superstition? "Progress means getting nearer to the place where you want to be," Lewis writes. "And if you have taken a wrong turning, then to go forward does not get you any nearer. If you are on the wrong road, progress means doing an about-turn and walking back to the right road. In that case the man who turns his back the soonest is the most progressive man." Going back, says Lewis, is the quickest way on.

Having reinforced his premise, Lewis returns to his original dichotomy, between the objective law of human nature and the human beings who constantly disobey the law. Here, Lewis says, lies the way of Christianity. "Christianity tells people to repent and promises them forgiveness. It therefore has nothing to say to people who do not know they have done anything to repent of and who do not feel that they need any forgiveness." The medicine of Christianity, in brief, only benefits those who realize that they are sick.

The second part of *Mere Christianity* discusses several specific elements of the Christian life, where Lewis shows how it responds to the human condition, how it can save man despite his congenial inability to live up to the law that is etched in his nature. For instance, Lewis demonstrates the nature of evil as not a thing in itself, but rather the "absence of due good."

No one seeks badness for its own sake, Lewis points out. The thief steals for material possessions but material possessions are good in themselves. Even the most inexplicable human cruelty fails the test of intrinsic badness. "In real life people are cruel for one of two reasons — either because they are sadists, that is, because they have perversion which makes cruelty a cause of sensual pleasure to them; or else for the sake of something that they are going to get out of it, such as money, power or safety." But pleasure, wealth, power, security: these are all good as far as they go. Wickedness consists in pursuing them in the wrong way.

"Badness cannot succeed even in being bad in the same way in which goodness is good," Lewis writes. "Goodness is, so to speak, itself: badness is only spoiled goodness." This means that human beings who are wicked must have originally had impulses that were good in order to be able to pervert them. Deviation cannot exist without a norm. Already Lewis is approaching the idea of original sin as a primordial calamity that corrupted the initial sanctity of the human soul. In addition, he asks, "Do you now begin to see why Christianity has always said that the devil is a fallen angel? That is not a mere story for children. It is a real recognition of the fact that evil is a parasite, not an original thing."

How are men who fall so woefully short of keeping the law of human nature going to escape their predictable plight, which is isolation from that perfect being who embodies the norms of goodness? How are we to avoid damnation? Here Lewis introduces that strange man who suddenly turned up among the Jews "talking as if He were God." Not only that, but he actually claimed to be God. Not "one with God" or "part of God" in the Buddhist or pantheist sense. He was a Jew, and in the monotheistic tradition in which Christ claimed to be God ("I and the Father are One"), he implied that he had existed from the beginning of time. He claimed to forgive sins — not just offenses against himself, but sins against other people, indeed sins against humanity.

"You tread on my toe and I forgive you, you steal my money and I forgive you," Lewis writes. "But what should we make of a man, himself unrobbed and untrod-

174

den on, who announced that he forgave you for treading on other people's toes and stealing other men's money? Yet this is what Jesus did. He told people that their sins were forgiven, and never waited to consult all other people whom their sins had undoubtedly injured. He unhesitatingly behaved as if He were the party chiefly concerned, the person chiefly offended in all offenses."

Then, in a stirring passage, Lewis sums up the choice about Christ that faces us all: "I am trying," Lewis says, "to prevent anyone saying the really foolish thing that people often say of Christ — I'm ready to accept Jesus as a great moral teacher, but I don't accept His claim to be God. This is the one thing we must not say. A man who was merely a man and said the sort of things Jesus said would not be a great moral teacher. He would be either a lunatic — on a level with the man who says he is a poached egg — or else he would be the Devil of Hell. You must make your choice. Either this man was, and is, the Son of God: or else a madman or something worse. You can shut Him up for a fool, you can spit at Him and kill Him as a demon; or you can fall at His feet and call Him Lord and God. But let us not come up with any patronizing nonsense about His being a great human teacher. He has not left that open to us. He did not intend to."

Christianity, Lewis says, offers man an explanation for his predicament and a way out of it, which is Christ. It is a matter of historical record that Christ's word is recorded in the Bible, and in the apostolic tradition established by Christ through Peter. "Do not be scared by the word Authority," Lewis writes, directing people to the sources of God's law and his truth. "Believing things on authority only means believing them because you have been told them by someone you think trustworthy." Lewis gives the example of countless facts — from the solar system, to atoms, to the circulation of blood — that few of us have actually seen, but we accept them because reputable and believable people say so. This is also true of history: Which of us was present at the Battle of Waterloo or the American Civil War? Yet no one doubts that these happened. Lewis's point is that authority is a sensible and practical way to acquire wisdom that is difficult, if not impossible, to glean from experience. In the case of Christianity, experience *confirms* the knowledge that we discover in the Bible and Church teaching, giving that knowledge a credibility and reality in our lives.

Lewis has some powerful insights into the application of Christian principles to life. Since it is impossible to improve on them, it is best to let Lewis's words speak directly to the reader:

On clergy involvement in politics: "People say — the Church ought to give us a lead. . . . By the Church they ought to mean the whole body of practicing Christians. But of course most people mean they want the clergy to put out a political program. That is silly. The clergy are those particular people within the whole Church who have been specifically trained and set aside to look after what concerns us as creatures who are going to live forever, and we are asking them to do quite a different job for which they have not been trained. The job is really on us, the laymen. The application of Christian principles to trade unionism or education must come from Christian trade unionists and Christian schoolmasters, just as Christian literature comes from Christian novelists and dramatists — not from the bench of bishops getting together and trying to write novels and plays in their spare time."

On sexual morality: "Christianity is almost the only one of the great religions which thoroughly approves the body — which believes that matter is good, that God himself once took a human body, that some kind of body is going to be given to us in Heaven. . . . But our sex instinct has gone wrong. The biological purpose of sex is children, just as the biological purpose of eating is to repair the body. Now one man may eat enough for two, but he does not eat enough for ten. The appetite goes a little beyond its biological purpose, but not enormously. But if a healthy man indulged his sexual appetite whenever he felt inclined, and if each act produced a baby, then in ten years he might easily populate a small village. The appetite is in ludicrous and preposterous excess of its function.

"Imagine: you can get a large audience together for a strip-tease act, that is, to watch a girl undress on stage. Now suppose you came to a country where you could fill a theatre by simply bringing a covered plate on to the stage and then slowly lifting the cover so as to let everyone see, just before the lights went out, that it contained a mutton chop or a bit of bacon, would not you think that in that country something had gone wrong with the appetite of food?

"The Christian idea of marriage is based on Christ's words that a man and wife are to be regarded as a single organism — one flesh. The monstrosity of sexual intercourse outside marriage is that those who indulge in it are trying to isolate one kind of union — the sexual — from all other kinds of union which were intended to go along with it and make up the total union. The Christian attitude does not mean that there is anything wrong about sexual pleasure, any more than about the pleasure of eating. It means that you must not isolate that pleasure and try to get it by itself, any more than you ought to try to get the pleasures of taste without swallowing and

177

digesting, by chewing things and then spitting them out again."

On faith and good works: "The sense in which a Christian leaves it to God is that he puts all his trust in Christ: trusts that Christ will somehow share with him the perfect human obedience which He carried out from His birth to His crucifixion. . . . Christ offers him something for nothing; He even offers everything for nothing. In a sense the whole Christian life consists in accepting that very remarkable offer. But the difficulty is to reach the point of recognizing that all we have done and can do is nothing.

"To trust him means, of course, trying to do all that He says. There would be no sense in saying that you trusted a person if you would not take his advice. Christians have often disputed as to whether what leads the Christian home is good actions, or faith in Christ. It seems to me like asking which blade in a pair of scissors is necessary.

"Good and evil both increase at compound interest. That is why the little decisions you and I make every day are of such infinite importance. The smallest good act today is the capture of a strategic point from which, a few months later, you may be able to go on to victories you never dreamed of. An apparently trivial indulgence in lust or anger today is the loss of a ridge or railway line or bridgehead from which the enemy may launch an attack otherwise impossible."

What beauty there is in these words, and what simplicity. Even as he expounds fine points of doctrine Lewis never loses the big picture. Doctrine, he says, is a kind of road map. We need the map in order to make our pilgrimage. The map is based on the collective experience of thousands who have gone before us, seeking what we seek and finding the right road. At the same time we should not confuse the map for the destination. Doctrine is the means to the end, which is the love of God.

Churches, Lewis says, are not the same thing as truth. Churches, too, are a means to arrive at the truth. The role of the Church is analogous to the role of the state, properly conceived. "The state exists simply to promote and protect the ordinary happiness of human beings in this life. . . . In the same way the Church exists for nothing else but to draw men to Christ, to make them little Christs. If they are not doing that, all the cathedrals, clergy, missions, sermons, even the Bible itself, are a waste of time."

Lewis's concluding point is that we should not expect salvation merely for exercising the fashionable social sentiments and the regimen of the professionally compassionate. "We must not suppose that even if we succeeded in making everyone nice, we should have saved their souls. A world of nice people, content in their own niceness, looking no further, turned away from God, would be just as desperately in need of salvation as a miserable world — and might even be more difficult to save."

Instead what Christianity calls us to is the total surrender of our lives to Christ, so that he may transform us according to his will and his image. "Imagine yourself as a living house. God comes in to rebuild that house. At first, perhaps, you can understand what He is doing. He is getting the drains right and stopping the leaks in the roof and so on; you knew that those jobs needed doing and so you are not surprised. But presently He starts knocking the house about in a way that hurts abominably and does not seem to make sense. What on earth is He up to? The explanation is that He is building quite a different house from the one you thought of — throwing out a new wing here, putting on an extra floor there, running up towers, making courtyards. You thought you were going to be made into a decent little cottage, but He is building a palace. He intends to come and live in it Himself."